Caen 1944

Montgomery's break-out attempt

Campaign • 143

Caen 1944

Montgomery's break-out attempt

Ken Ford • Illustrated by Peter Dennis

First published in Great Britain in 2004 by Osprey Publishing,
Midland House, West Way, Botley, Oxford OX2 0PH, UK
443 Park Avenue South, New York, NY 10016, USA
Email: info@ospreypublishing.com

A CIP catalogue record for this book is available from the British Library

ISBN 978 1 84176 625 6

Editor: Lee Johnson
Design: The Black Spot
Index by David Worthington
Maps by The Map Studio
3D bird's-eye views by The Black Spot
Battlescene artwork by Peter Dennis
Originated by The Electronic Page Company, Cwmbran, UK
Printed in China through World Print Ltd.
Typeset in Helvetica Neue and ITC New Baskerville

08 09 10 11 12 13 12 11 10 9 8 7 6 5 4

For a catalogue of all books published by Osprey Military
and Aviation please contact:

NORTH AMERICA
Osprey Direct, C/o Random House Distribution
Center, 400 Hahn Road, Westminster, MD 21157, USA
E-mail: info@ospreydirect.com

ALL OTHER REGIONS
Osprey Direct UK, P.O. Box 140,
Wellingborough, Northants, NN8 2FA, UK
E-mail: info@ospreydirect.co.uk

www.ospreypublishing.com

Artist's note

Readers may care to note that the original paintings from
which the colour plates in this book were prepared are
available for private sale. All reproduction copyright
whatsoever is retained by the Publishers. All enquiries
should be addressed to:

Peter Dennis
Fieldhead
The Park
Mansfield
Notts
NG18 2AT

The Publishers regret that they can enter into no
correspondence upon this matter.

KEY TO MILITARY SYMBOLS

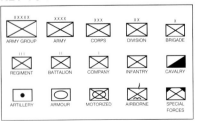

CONTENTS

FIRST ALLIED MOVES ON CAEN

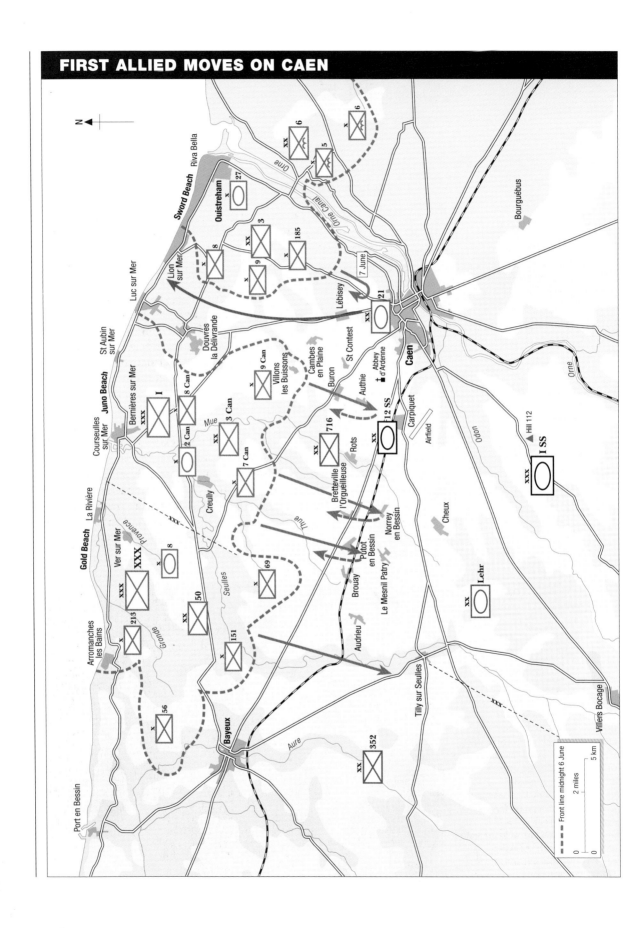

ORIGINS OF THE BATTLE

On 7 April 1944, General Bernard Montgomery, Commander 21st Army Group, briefed all the senior commanders involved in the forthcoming landings in France on the final shape of the invasion plan. Operation Overlord, as the invasion was called, proposed that two Allied armies be landed on the coast of Normandy between the mouth of the River Orne and the base of the Cotentin Peninsula to establish a lodgement from which future operations inland would develop. Montgomery went on to explain how the build-up of troops and equipment would progress and how the growing forces would be used, outlining proposals for the expansion of the beachhead and the preparations required to resist the inevitable German counterattacks. One of the keys to the success of his plans, he told them, was the early capture of the city of Caen and its vital road and rail communications.

Caen is situated astride the River Orne 12 kilometres (7.46 miles) inland from the coast and is linked to the sea by the river and a ship canal. In 1944 it was the regional capital of Calvados, surrounded by rich undulating farmland. It also had a large industrial area on the outskirts of the city on the eastern side of the Orne that was dominated by the giant steelworks at Colombelles. Radiating from Caen was a network of road and rail lines leading west towards the Cotentin peninsula and Brittany, east towards Le Havre and the River Seine and inland to the interior of France. This nexus of road and rail links was vital to Allied plans for the drive inland from the beaches.

Panzergrenadiers of Battlegroup von Luck from 21st Panzer Division, on the southern outskirts of Caen just before the start of Operation Goodwood. Oberst von Luck was commander of 125th Panzergrenadier Regiment of the division and had formed this battlegroup from the depleted members of his regiment who had been in almost daily contact with the Allies since D-Day. (Bundesarchiv 1011/722/0405/04)

One of the D-Day beaches given over to the landing of stores after the assault. Most of the stores and equipment used by the Allies in the battle for Normandy were landed over open beaches. These supplies still continued to come ashore here even when the Allies had broken out of the region and were almost at the German border. (IWM CL 537)

The early capture of the city was one of the prime objectives of the British troops who landed on D-Day. British 3rd Division, commanded by Major-General Rennie, made an assault landing over 'Sword' Beach on 6 June 1944 to herald the start of the invasion. The division was reinforced by the tanks of 27th Armoured Brigade and was ordered to drive on Caen and capture it with all speed, with its right flank protected by Canadian 3rd Division landing on the adjacent 'Juno' Beach. Montgomery wanted Caen's bridges over the Orne in the centre of the city to be in British hands by the end of the day. In the event, British 3rd Division could get no closer than seven kilometres to those bridges on D-Day. The division lacked the drive needed to make such a bold move and a German counterattack by 21st Panzer Division forced it to dig into positions north of the city where it remained for the next four weeks.

With hindsight, the expectation that a single division could capture Caen on D-Day was perhaps overambitious, especially with a German Panzer division located just to the south of the city within a few hours' march of the sea. The capture of Caen quickly became an even more difficult proposition when the first German armoured reinforcements to be moved against the landings were put into the line around Caen. The arrival of the 12th SS-Panzer Division 'Hitlerjugend' and the elite Panzer Lehr Division, both well-equipped and with excellent morale, just two days after the Allied landings ensured that the British and Canadians faced a bitter struggle for control of the city.

Both sides considered the possession of Caen to be the cornerstone of their strategy in Normandy. To Montgomery, the capture of the city was a prerequisite for his advance onto the open plain to the south where he could deploy his armoured divisions to force a breakthrough towards Paris and the south-east. This was his original plan, outlined before the invasion, which he modified as his forces struggled unsuccessfully, week after week, to seize the city. He subsequently adapted his strategy, suggesting that he continue to batter at Caen, threatening a breakthrough and all the while drawing more of the German armour onto his front, ultimately allowing

An aerial view of the centre of Caen showing the River Orne running through the city from bottom to top. The Caen canal and its lock gates are in the top left of the picture. Evidence of the early bombing can be seen near the river at lower left, but all three bridges are still intact. (National Archives of Canada C104861)

the Americans to effect a breakthrough further to the west against less formidable German forces.

Montgomery launched a number of discrete operations aimed at capturing Caen. The first attempt to take the city was nothing more sophisticated than a headlong dash from the beaches. When this failed he tried sending an armoured division in a wide encircling movement around to the south of the city to cut its communications and supply lines to the interior. This move was combined with another more direct thrust by the Highland Division out of the original 6th Airborne Division bridgehead east of the Orne. Both failed well short of their objectives. Montgomery tried again with a full corps in a set piece attack to push behind the city from the west with no greater success. The next operation attempted to bludgeon its way directly into the city centre along the shortest route with three infantry divisions, supported by the full weight of RAF Bomber Command. Caen was reduced to rubble in the operation and although the centre of the city was secured, the key objective, the bridges across the River Orne, remained beyond reach. It took three armoured divisions, three infantry divisions and several independent armoured brigades, together with the heavy, medium and fighter-bombers of the RAF and the USAAF, in the largest of all the Caen-related operations to finally capture the entire city. British forces swept around the eastern side of Caen and the Canadians encircled it from the west, eventually squeezing German forces from the city completely, opening the roads to the south-west. Caen was a Pyrrhic victory, however, with the city left a shattered wasteland of smoking rubble and the enemy's Panzer forces still gathered in strength to the south, barring Montgomery's way onto the Falaise plain.

CHRONOLOGY

6 June D-DAY. Allied forces land in Normandy beginning the liberation of France. The Americans land US First Army on the western beaches 'Omaha' and 'Utah', whilst the British land their Second Army on 'Gold', 'Juno' and 'Sword' beaches to the east. British 3rd Division and Canadian 3rd Division advance inland from 'Sword' and 'Juno' beaches to capture Caen and its airfield at Carpiquet. This move is halted by a German counterattack by 21st Panzer Division that pushes between 'Sword' and 'Juno' beaches as far as the coast.

7 June Canadian and British 3rd Divisions resume their advance on Caen, but both are halted once more by the arrival of 12th SS-Panzer Division 'Hitlerjugend'.

8–11 June While British 3rd Division holds its line, the Canadians attempt to enlarge their beachhead to the west of Caen but are frustrated by counterattacks by 12th SS-Panzer Division.

12 June 51st Highland Division fails in an attempt to push around Caen from the east. 7th Armoured Division attempts a wide encirclement to the west of the city, but suffers heavily in an ambush at Villers-Bocage at the hands of several PzKpfw VI Tiger I tanks commanded by Hauptsturmführer Michael Wittmann. The division is halted in its tracks and subsequently withdrawn back into XXX Corps' line south of Bayeux.

18 June A great storm hits the Channel coast and destroys the American Mulberry harbour and damages the British artificial port at Arromanches. The storm blows for four days disrupting the build-up for Montgomery's proposed new offensive.

25 June XXX Corps starts preliminary moves to seize high ground around Rauray to protect the left flank of VIII Corps on its advance to the Odon.

26–29 June OPERATION EPSOM carves out a salient in the enemy line and wins a bridgehead over the River Odon, but fails in its objective of crossing the River Orne and securing the high ground astride the Caen–Falaise road. 11th Armoured Division gets tanks onto Hill 112 but is later forced to withdraw.

1 July The big German counterattack against the landings fails to generate enough punch to penetrate the salient gained by VIII Corps. The impact of fresh armoured reinforcements is lost as they have to be fed into the battle piecemeal to prevent the Allies piercing the German line.

2 July Generalfeldmarschall von Rundstedt is dismissed as German Commander-in-Chief (West) for daring to suggest to Hitler that Caen be given up and a new position be established on a more easily defended line.

4–5 July OPERATION WINDSOR launched by Canadian 3rd Division to capture Carpiquet village and its airfield. The heavily-fortified site protects the western approaches to Caen and, despite terrible casualties, 12th SS-Panzer Division refuses to loosen its grip on the area. The operation is halted on the second day with the only gain being the now utterly destroyed village of Carpiquet.

8–9 July OPERATION CHARNWOOD begins with heavy bomber raids on the northern outskirts of Caen. Three infantry divisions of I Corps attack the city in a mighty show of strength that leaves Caen a mass of burning rubble. The northern part of the city is taken, but the bridges over the River Orne in the south of Caen remain in enemy hands.

10 July A strengthened 43rd Division launches OPERATION JUPITER to capture Hill 112 and get to the River Orne. Hill 112 is taken after two days of fighting and then given up in the face of intense German resistance from 9th and 10th SS-Panzer Divisions. The 43rd Division suffers over 2,000 casualties in the two-day battle.

15–17 July Montgomery orders Dempsey to resume attacks along the Odon front with XII and XXX Corps in order to keep enemy armour engaged whilst he organises a major new offensive on the eastern side of the River Orne out of the airborne bridgehead. These attacks gain little new ground and suffer 3,500 casualties, but the pressure forces General der Panzertruppen Eberbach of Panzer Group West to commit more of his armour against them.

18 July Montgomery launches OPERATION GOODWOOD with Canadian II, British I and VIII Corps, planning to send three armoured divisions southwards to establish themselves on the high ground astride the Caen–Falaise road. After the largest bombing raid ever mounted in support of ground troops, the three corps launch their attacks. Initially progress is good, but German anti-tank guns on the Bourguébus Ridge and in the adjacent fortified villages bring the armoured divisions' advance to a halt.

19 July Attacking out of the centre of Caen and from the area west of the city, Canadian 2nd Division pushes across the River Orne. After fierce fighting they link up with Canadian 3rd Division completing the encirclement of Caen. The city is finally completely in Allied hands 36 days after the landings.

20 July OPERATION GOODWOOD is halted with the Allied armoured divisions still well short of the Caen–Falaise road.

OPPOSING COMMANDERS

LtGen Richard O'Connor (left), Commander VIII Corps and LtGen Sir Miles Dempsey (right), Commander British Second Army just before the Goodwood offensive. (IWM B6956)

BRITISH COMMANDERS

General Sir Bernard Law Montgomery had gained an impressive reputation as a result of his campaigns in North Africa and the Mediterranean. The string of victories that followed his triumph at El Alamein in November 1942 made him the obvious choice to lead the invasion forces on their return to France under the Supreme Command of General Dwight D. Eisenhower. Montgomery was suspicious of the abilities of many other British commanders and chose to have under him those that he had already fought with in North Africa, Sicily and Italy. To head British Second Army he selected **Lieutenant-General Sir Miles Dempsey** who had commanded XIII Corps in Montgomery's Eighth Army in North Africa and the Mediterranean. The commanders of the two British corps that carried out the assault were also officers who had served in the Mediterranean. **Lieutenant-General Gerard Bucknall** commanded British XXX Corps and had been a divisional commander with Eighth Army. Montgomery had been impressed with his performance in handling 5th Division in Sicily and Italy and recommended him for promotion to corps commander in 1943. Field Marshal Alan Brooke, Chief of the Imperial General Staff and Montgomery's boss, thought that Bucknall was unsuitable for such an appointment. Alan Brooke was later proved right, and Bucknall was relieved of his command of XXX Corps in early August. **Lieutenant-General John Crocker**, Commander British I Corps, was a veteran of the North African campaigns having commanded IX Corps in Tunisia in the less than highly regarded First Army of Lieutenant-General

LtGen Sir Miles Dempsey (left), Commander Second Army, General Sir Bernard Montgomery (centre), Commander 21st Army Group and LtGen Guy Simmonds (right), Commander Canadian II Corps. (M. Dean, NAC PA 131258)

Kenneth Anderson. Despite this he was still brought home to England in 1943 to command I Corps specifically for the invasion.

These three senior commanders oversaw the first few battles in Normandy after the landings. They were joined in mid-June by **Lieutenant-General Sir Richard O'Connor**, a remarkable commander who had served with Wavell in the early desert battles in North Africa. O'Connor had achieved a reputation for bold action and swift movement during the fighting against the Italians and had scored some notable victories. He was captured by the Italians in April 1942, but escaped almost a year later and returned to England. O'Connor was given command of VIII Corps, which was to land in the weeks following the invasion.

As the lodgement was enlarged, more units were landed in Normandy. In July, **Lieutenant-General Neil Ritchie** arrived with his XII Corps. Ritchie had at one time been commander of Eighth Army in North Africa before Monty, but was dismissed by his then boss, General Sir Claude Auchinleck, after Rommel's victory at Gazala and the loss of Tobruk. Back in England he was given command of 52nd Lowland Division. At the beginning of 1944 he rose to command XII Corps, which was in training as a follow-up corps for the Normandy campaign.

Lieutenant-General Guy Simmonds gained himself a remarkable reputation after having fought with Canadian 1st Infantry and 5th Armoured Divisions in Sicily and Italy as part of Eighth Army. He arrived back in England from the Mediterranean in January 1944 and was given command of Canadian II Corps. Just one Canadian division was involved in the landings when Canadian 3rd Division, commanded by Major-General Rod Keller, landed on 'Juno' Beach on D-Day as part of British I Corps. Providing this division with armoured support was Canadian 2nd Armoured Brigade. Further Canadian units, 2nd Infantry Division and 4th Armoured Division, transferred to France in July. It had been intended that all Canadian forces would serve in Canadian First Army in Normandy, but this army could not be made operational until the front was sufficiently advanced to provide room for its deployment.

LtGen Neil Ritchie, Commander XII Corps, in late July 1944. Ritchie had at one time commanded Eighth Army in North Africa under Auchinleck, but was dismissed after the battle of Gazala and the loss of Tobruk. (IWM B8222)

Generalfeldmarschall Gerd von Rundstedt, C-in-C (West) on a visit to 12th SS-Panzer Division 'Hitlerjugend' before the invasion. From left to right: von Rundstedt, Standartenführer Kurt Meyer, commander 25th SS-Panzergrenadiers, Brigadeführer Fritz Witt, commander 12th SS-Panzer Division, Obergruppenführer Josef 'Sepp' Dietrich, commander I SS-Panzer Corps. (Bundesarchiv)

Generalfeldmarschall Günther von Kluge who took over command as Commander-in-Chief (West) from von Rundstedt in early July. Von Kluge commanded Fourth Army in France and Russia, then replaced Bock in command of Army Group Centre. Von Kluge performed extremely well in Russia and became one of Hitler's favourite field commanders. (IWM GER 1276)

Obergruppenführer Wilhelm Bittrich, commander II SS-Panzer Corps. Bittrich had led both 2nd SS-Panzer Division 'Das Reich' and 9th SS-Panzer Division 'Hohenstaufen' in Russia before coming to the west and taking command of II SS-Panzer Corps in Normandy. He rose to particular prominence in September 1944 when he was responsible for wiping out the British bridgehead at Arnhem. (Bundesarchiv 146/1971/033/51)

Until then, the Canadian forces formed Canadian II Corps and served as part of British Second Army.

The battles to take Caen involved all five of those Second Army corps that had arrived in Normandy. The divisions serving in those corps were a mix of battle-hardened veterans and untried new formations. Montgomery wanted some of the army's best divisions with him when he invaded France, tried and tested units under experienced commanders. He brought back from the Mediterranean several of the famous divisions that had gained proud reputations fighting with Eighth Army. Senior officers who had already proved themselves in action commanded these formations during the Normandy campaign. Men like **Major-General George Erskine** of 7th Armoured Division, the Desert Rats, who had led his division in North Africa and Sicily, and **Major-General Tom Rennie** of 51st Highland Division, who had commanded a battalion at El Alamein and a brigade in Sicily. Also leading divisions in Normandy were men promoted into command through their proven ability. **Major-General 'Pip' Roberts** led 11th Armoured Division by virtue of his reputation as a leader in North Africa, where he commanded both at battalion and brigade level in some of the heaviest fighting. At 38 years of age he was the youngest divisional commander in the British Army and went on to prove his worth in the subsequent campaigns in North-West Europe.

GERMAN COMMANDERS

By this point in the war, Hitler was not only titular head of the German Army, but had taken effective command of all German forces in the field. He involved himself in all major, and often very minor, decisions regarding the prosecution of the war. The dictator's continual interference in the strategy and deployment of his forces in Normandy left the German High Command in western Europe with a feeling of impotence. **Generalfeldmarschall Gerd von Rundstedt** was, as Commander-in-Chief (West), responsible to Oberkommando der Wehrmacht (OKW) in Berlin, but this in effect meant that he was answerable to Hitler himself. In principle, Von Rundstedt controlled all German forces in the west with Army Group B under **Generalfeldmarschall Erwin Rommel** occupying most of France and the Low Countries. Normandy came under **Generaloberst Friedrich Dollmann**, commander of German Seventh Army.

When the Allies landed in Normandy, they faced the static divisions of Dollmann's Seventh Army bolstered by a few good infantry divisions, such as 352nd Division, backed by the armour of 21st Panzer Division. As soon as the landings had been recognised as the invasion and not just a diversionary raid, further Panzer formations were released to Normandy by OKW. On 8 June 1944, Panzer Group West was made operational and took control of all armoured forces in Normandy. The I SS-Panzer Corps had been established the day before and sent into the line around Caen under the veteran Nazi **SS-Obergruppenführer Josef 'Sepp' Dietrich**, previous commander of the Führer's bodyguard, the 'Leibstandarte SS Adolf Hitler'. I SS-Panzer Corps consisted of 12th SS-Panzer (SS-Brigadeführer Fritz Witt), 21st Panzer (Generalmajor Edgar Feuchtinger) and Panzer Lehr (Generalmajor Hyazinth Strachwitz/ Generalleutnant Fritz Bayerlein) Divisions, together with the remnants of 716th Infantry Division (Generalleutnant Wilhelm Richter), which had been all but annihilated amid the ferocity of the Allied landings over 'Sword' and 'Juno' beaches. Panzer Group West was commanded by the aristocratic **General der Panzertruppen Leo Geyr Freiherr von Schweppenburg**, who had been a corps commander in France in 1940 and a Panzer corps commander in Russia in 1942–43. Just after the invasion, Allied intelligence gathered from 'Ultra' intercepts located on Schweppenburg's headquarters. The RAF launched a raid on his HQ in which the general was wounded and his entire headquarters staff virtually wiped out. The HQ remained inoperative until the end of June. The raid left Von Schweppenburg himself psychologically traumatised and in early July he was transferred to the reserve command, having run foul of Hitler.

The guns of **General der Flak Wolfgang Pickert**'s III Flak Corps were to be the cause of much grief to the Allied forces. Stationed in Normandy in an attempt to at least partly counter the overwhelming Allied air superiority, Pickert's guns were as often employed in a ground role as anti-tank weapons. As the British had discovered in North Africa, the formidable 88mm guns proved particularly effective in this role. The guns remained strictly under Luftwaffe control, however, with all important decisions, including deployment, made by Luftwaffe officers, a situation that led to friction and regular clashes with army officers.

General der Flak Wolfgang Pickert, Commander III Flak Corps. It was Pickert's dual-purpose 88mm guns that wreaked such havoc with British armour in Normandy, especially during Operation Goodwood. (Bundesarchiv 1011/493/3358/15A)

OPPOSING ARMIES

The Allied formations that fought the battles around Caen between 6 June and 20 July 1944, enjoyed a considerable superiority over their German opponents. They were properly equipped and organised, well trained and with high morale. Even in the most disrupted periods, supplies of basic necessities such as food, fuel and ammunition were available in sufficient quantity, and Allied air and naval support was overwhelming. By contrast, German units were often under strength, with limited supplies of fuel, stores, weapons and ammunition, and the voracious demands of the fighting in Russia had progressively stripped units in France of their best men. These had increasingly been replaced by foreign nationals, or at best *Volksdeutsche*, whose training, enthusiasm and morale were questionable. Allied air superiority depleted units before they ever reached the front line. With the landings in Normandy, the German Army was forced to fight a war on two fronts – a strategic nightmare. Assailed from both east and west and with the Fatherland being bombed remorselessly by day and night, many Germans saw the war as already lost.

The armies on both sides that fought during the battle for Caen contained a mix of seasoned divisions that had been involved in fighting in other theatres and new formations who had yet to see action. What the troops on both sides did have in common was that many of their commanders were experienced men promoted as a result of proven ability in combat. There was also a scattering of officers on both sides, however, who had seen little action, some not since the Great War,

RAF ground crews watch rocket-firing Typhoon aircraft taxiing out onto a grass runway for a daylight sortie. By the end of June the RAF had 11 airstrips operational in Normandy. (IWM CL403)

whose ideas were outdated or who lacked the boldness to take swift, decisive action. These failings would lead some units to perform below expectation.

THE BRITISH ARMY

The first two corps to arrive in Normandy, British I and XXX Corps, consisted of divisions that had been trained specifically for the invasion. In the case of two of the three assault divisions, British and Canadian 3rd Divisions, the action on 6 June was their first. The other assault division, British 50th Northumbrian Division, had seen action in North Africa in 1942 and had earned itself a reputation as a tough unit during the battles of Gazala and El Alamein. These three divisions had spent a great deal of their training concentrating on just breaking through the steel and concrete defences of Hitler's Atlantic Wall. D-Day and the storming of the beaches became their overriding consideration. On D-Day, in the immediate aftermath of overcoming the beach defences, it proved difficult to maintain the momentum of these units and not one of the three divisions achieved their final D-Day objectives.

The follow-up divisions started to arrive on the second tide on D-Day. Two of General Montgomery's veteran outfits from the desert were the next to enter the beachhead. The 51st Highland Division, of El Alamein fame, came ashore across 'Juno' Beach behind the Canadians, and 7th Armoured Division, the Desert Rats, followed 50th Division ashore on 'Gold' Beach. Several independent armoured brigades were already ashore, for tanks had landed with the assault divisions either 'swimming' in, as Duplex Drive (DD) amphibious tanks, or landing directly onto the beach from tank landing craft. The 8th Armoured Brigade landed on 6 June with 50th Division, Canadian 2nd Armoured Brigade was part of Canadian 3rd Division's assault on 'Juno' Beach and 27th Armoured Brigade came ashore with British 3rd Division on 'Sword' Beach.

Independent armoured brigades were essentially part of 21st Army Group's reserve. They had been trained for armoured operations, but were principally used to support infantry divisions during an attack. The armoured brigade was usually assigned to a corps, but often came under the command of a division and was able to work closely with the infantry, giving support as directed just where and when it was required. Some of these associations, such as that of 8th Armoured Brigade and 43rd Wessex Division, continued until the end of the war, with an individual regiment of the armoured brigade fighting regularly with a particular infantry brigade. In this way coordination and cooperation between units was enhanced.

Several independent armoured brigades served in Normandy: 4th, 8th, 27th, 33rd and Canadian 2nd Armoured Brigades. All of these brigades were equipped with Sherman cruiser tanks. There were also independent tank brigades assigned to

A Canadian 3in. mortar crew from the Regina Rifles in action near Bretteville L'Orgueilleuse to the south of Caen. (Donald Grant, NAC PA 128794)

A German aid station near Caen. This ambulance has to be driven into a bombproof trench to escape the attention of Allied fighter-bombers when not in use, even though it is clearly marked with the Red Cross. (Bundesarchiv 1011/495/3435/25A)

21st Army Group. These contained the heavier Churchill infantry tanks. Those serving in Normandy were 6th Guards Tank Brigade and the 31st and 34th Tank Brigade.

Once the lodgement in Normandy had expanded sufficiently to allow further formations to be landed, LtGen Richard O'Connor's VIII Corps was activated. Its divisions landed in mid-June and were ready for their first operation by the 26th. The corps eventually contained four divisions, all untried in battle: 15th Scottish, 43rd Wessex, 53rd Welsh and 11th Armoured. Two of the divisions were led by commanders with recent battle experience. 15th Scottish Division was commanded by MajGen Gordon MacMillan who had commanded 152nd Brigade of the Highland Division in Sicily. The youthful MajGen G.P.B. 'Pip' Roberts was at the head of 11th Armoured Division. 43rd Wessex Division was commanded by an ex-Royal Artillery officer, MajGen G. I Thomas, who had not seen action since the First World War where he had won and MC and DSO. MajGen R.K. Ross, who had commanded 160th Brigade in England before he took over 53rd Division, was also yet to see action.

Canadian 2nd Division, commanded by MajGen C. Foulkes, joined Canadian 3rd Division and Canadian 2nd Armoured Brigade in Normandy in early July. Its arrival allowed Canadian II Corps to be formed under the leadership of LtGen Guy Simmonds, the fourth corps to join the struggle in the British sector. The Canadian troops in France were all volunteers; in Canada conscripts were raised for national defence and were exempted from service overseas unless they volunteered. Those Canadian forces serving overseas would remain overwhelmingly a volunteer force throughout the war.

XII Corps was also raised at the beginning of July under the command of LtGen Neil Ritchie. Its first attack was on 15 July, when it took over three divisions previously under VIII Corps command. Attacking to the south-east from the ground taken during Operation Epsom, British XII Corps sought to tie down German forces to the west of Caen prior to the Goodwood armoured offensive to the east of the city.

During late June, two more British divisions joined Second Army in Normandy. Both divisions, Guards Armoured under MajGen A. Adair and 59th Staffordshire commanded by MajGen L.O. Lyne, were yet to see

17

A Sherman tank from
29th Armoured Brigade, part
of the 11th Armoured Division.
The signpost shows that the
location is just to the north of
the River Odon. (IWM B6980)

action having spent the whole of the war thus far in England. The 59th
Division had a very brief active life; it began to come ashore in Normandy
on 27 June, was sent into army reserve on 21 August and disbanded on
18 October 1944.

All of the divisions fighting in the early battles in Normandy began
the campaign at full strength and with their full complement of vehicles
and armaments. As the fighting degenerated into a grinding war of
attrition with advances measured in yards, British units paid a heavy
price in casualties. Although Allied industrial might could replace
matériel losses swiftly, Britain was finding it increasingly difficult to
maintain manpower levels. Compared to some of the other combatants,
particularly the United States, Britain's population was relatively small.
She had been at war continuously since September 1939, fighting in
a number of theatres across the globe. The burden of replacing combat
casualties was becoming increasingly onerous. The high level of losses
sustained in the first month of fighting in Normandy, showed that a
manpower crisis was developing. Either a way must be found to reduce
casualties, perhaps involving a more cautious approach to operations, or
men would have to be stripped from the other services and retrained
as infantry. Finally, existing divisions could be disbanded and their
men used to bolster other units. This would reduce Britain's role in the
fighting and inevitably its influence over the conduct of the war. All of
these solutions were anathema to Montgomery, but nonetheless they
were all gradually implemented as the war continued.

Britain did not have the same difficulties with regard to maintaining
stocks of matériel. Ammunition for the guns was plentiful, allowing
the 25-pdrs to lay down a prodigious barrage in support of every attack
and to intervene just as effectively against enemy attacks. Tanks, most
especially Shermans, were rapidly replaced from the huge numbers now
being produced by the United States. The Allies' logistics machinery was

operating with great efficiency, allowing their commanders to choose when, where and how they would strike the enemy.

Formed in June 1943 in preparation for Operation Overlord, Air Marshal Arthur Coningham's 2nd Tactical Air Force (2nd TAF) was to attack specific enemy targets of tactical significance and provide British 2nd Army with ground-attack air support. During the air campaign that preceded the invasion itself 2nd TAF attacked the German road and rail networks in France, bombed key bridges and attacked troop concentrations, and on D-Day itself provided a protective aerial umbrella while the beachhead was established. Within four days of the landings 2nd TAF had airstrips operational in France.

RAF 2nd Tactical Airforce consisted of four groups: No 2 Group Bomber Command with 12 squadrons of light and medium bomber aircraft; No. 83rd Composite Group containing 34 reconnaissance, air observation, fighter and fighter-bomber squadrons; No. 84 Composite Group with a similar mix of 31 squadrons; and No. 85 Base Group with 21½ day- and night-fighter squadrons, photo-reconnaissance squadrons and Fleet Air Arm and RAF air spotting pool squadrons.

THE GERMAN ARMY

As with the British forces, German divisions in the Caen sector included a mixture of experienced and green units. The sector of the coast where British Second Army landed was held by Generalleutnant Wilhelm Richter's 716th Division. This division was a static formation raised for garrison duties in occupied countries and consisted of just two infantry regiments and three battalions of artillery. On 6 June 1944 the over-whelming force and ferocity of the Allied attack meant that the division had all but ceased to exist by the end of the day. Its personnel were far from being first-rate troops, including many foreigners conscripted into the service of the Third Reich. Housed in concrete and steel fortifications, its role was to slow down the assault to allow other formations to come forward and seal off any Allied breakthrough. Richter's men did slow down the assault as planned on D-Day, but supporting units failed to arrive quickly enough or in sufficient strength.

The 21st Panzer Division, commanded by Generalmajor Edgar Feuchtinger, was deployed just south of Caen on D-Day under local command and was intended to move against any landings in the Normandy area. During the early hours of 6 June the division was directed against the airborne landings east of the Orne. This proved to be something of a wild-goose chase and left the unit unable to intervene against the Anglo-Canadian landings at 'Sword' and 'Juno' beaches until much later in the day. Thus when British I Corps came ashore that morning between Ouistreham and Lion sur Mer, the Panzer division had to switch its axis of advance from the east to the west of Caen and it was not until 16.00hrs that it could move in any force against the British on the beaches. Its attack failed with just a few tanks and Panzergrenadiers pushing through to the coast.

The 21st Panzer Division was a mere shadow of the crack formation it had been fighting under Rommel in the Western Desert and at El Alamein. Destroyed during the subsequent Axis collapse in North Africa, it was re-formed in Normandy in July 1943. Its ranks included many who would have been considered unacceptable by other divisions and it had equipment to match, its tanks being largely obsolete early-model Panzerkampfwagen IVs and captured French tanks.

The first significant German reinforcements to arrive in the Caen area consisted of 12th SS-Panzer Division 'Hitlerjugend' led by SS-Brigade-führer Fritz Witt and Generalleutnant Fritz Bayerlein's Panzer Lehr Division. These were both well-equipped units[1] with first-rate personnel although, in terms of combat experience, Normandy would be something of a baptism of fire for both. The commitment and morale of the men of both units was unquestioned; 'Hitlerjugend' had been recruited from the ranks of the Hitler Youth movement with a leavening of experienced officers and NCOs from 1st SS-Panzer Division 'Leibstandarte SS Adolf Hitler'. Panzer Lehr, as its name implied, was formed from the Panzer demonstration units of the various armoured warfare schools around Germany, giving its personnel an unusually high level of expertise. Both units had large establishments of the best available equipment – their tanks included latest variants of the Panzerkampfwagen IV, and PzKpfw V Panthers and VI Tigers, and their Panzergrenadiers were motorised, as was the bulk of their supporting artillery. On paper, the arrival of these two powerful formations should have given Rommel the necessary punch to overwhelm the still precarious British beachhead.

That this did not happen is symptomatic of several problems that were to bedevil German operations in Normandy. Firstly, with all road and rail movement subject to interdiction by Allied air power, particularly in daylight, it took days for these units to reach the front and then they arrived piecemeal, in dribs and drabs, rather than in formed units. Secondly, even when they reached the Normandy front, there was no chance to group these units into a powerful single force and employ them en masse. Rather they were fed into the line in 'penny packets' to avert a local crisis or bolster a threatened section of the front. From the first moment they confronted the British and Canadians, these powerful divisions found themselves fighting a defensive campaign rather than acting as an armoured spearhead to drive the Allies into the sea.

It was the same story with practically every German division sucked into the maelstrom in Normandy. As each arrived they were fed in their turn into the meatgrinder. The pressure exerted by Montgomery to seize Caen and to break out onto the flat terrain south of the city drew the strongest of the German formations against him. Hitler remained unconvinced that the landings in Normandy were the Allies' primary effort and for some considerable time clung to the belief that further, stronger landings would take place in the Pas de Calais area opposite the Straits of Dover. As a result almost the whole of German Fifteenth Army remained guarding the Calais region, perfectly positioned to counter an attack that would never come. To deal with the growing threat in Normandy, Hitler stripped units from other areas of France and the Low Countries and from the struggle in Russia, including four more powerful SS divisions – 1st SS-Panzer Division 'Leibstandarte', 2nd SS-Panzer Division 'Das Reich', 9th SS-Panzer Division 'Hohenstaufen' and 10th SS-Panzer Division 'Frundsberg', with the last three combining to form II SS-Panzer Corps.

---

[1] Panzer Lehr was stationed near Paris on D-Day and had a very large establishment of 190 tanks, 40 assault guns and more than 600 half-tracks.

OPPOSING PLANS

The allies had landed in Normandy beneath the protective umbrella of overwhelming air and naval support. A major aerial campaign waged against the French road and rail network, in advance of the landings, had reduced its capacity by around 60 per cent, with a commensurate reduction in the German army's ability to re-deploy troops effectively. The need to defend the heart of the Reich against the intensifying strategic bombing campaign had drawn off much of the Luftwaffe's strength in France and what was left had been targeted by aggressive Allied fighter sweeps across France and the Low Countries. The net result was that the Luftwaffe units still defending France were mere shadows of their former selves. There were no major German naval assets assigned to the ports of northern France and those units of the Kriegsmarine stationed in the Normandy area (mostly S- and E-Boats) were incapable of engaging the Allied armada in any effective manner. Once the landings had taken place, this Allied domination of the air and the sea had perforce to be extended to the fields of Normandy if a breakout was to be achieved.

A foothold in France, however secure, was but a first step in the liberation of France and the destruction of the Third Reich. Allied Supreme Commander General Dwight Eisenhower knew that to end the war his forces would have to fight their way into the heart of the Nazi Empire. The beachhead was just a springboard for further operations that would have three main objectives. First, the beachhead would have

A 25-pdr field gun of the 49th Division joins in the barrage being laid to support troops of other divisions in their attack on Caen on 8 July. The gun was the mainstay of the divisional artillery and its accomplished crews were able to keep up such a prodigious rate of fire that some of the enemy troops thought that the gun must be semi-automatic. (IWM B6578)

to be expanded to secure enough ground for the follow-up divisions to be landed and the build-up to be completed. Allied superiority in numbers and matériel would be meaningless unless sufficient real estate could be secured on which to deploy these forces. Second, the main German forces must be drawn into battle where this Allied superiority could be brought to bear decisively. Only then could the Allies break out from their enclave in Normandy into the heartland of France and begin the destruction of Hitler's 'Thousand Year Reich'.

BRITISH PLANS

Before the invasion, Gen Montgomery had stressed the importance of the early capture of Caen. Indeed his plans for D-Day ambitiously included the seizure of the city and the bridges over the River Orne. By nightfall on 6 June he hoped to have troops and armour from British 3rd Division and 27th Armoured Brigade on the road network to the south of Caen, while to the west of the city Canadian 3rd Division would be astride the road and rail lines from Caen to Bayeux, overlooking Carpiquet airfield. Yet further west, British 50th Division would be in Bayeux and have linked up with the Canadians along those same road and rail lines. A further infantry division and an armoured division would land the next day to strengthen this bridgehead, ready to receive the first inevitable enemy counterattack. Once the enemy response had been blunted by a combination of artillery, air attacks and naval gunfire, the advance would continue and more ground would be taken to allow additional formations to land and deploy. By this time the enemy would have brought forward his reserve Panzer divisions and organised them for a big push against the landings. Montgomery's intention was that this would not be allowed to happen. He planned to apply continual pressure all along the line, maintaining the strategic and operational initiative and forcing the enemy to react to his moves. The Germans

Men of 5th Duke of Cornwall's Light Infantry, 214th Brigade, 43rd Wessex Division, dig slit trenches on the edge of a field near Verson during Operation Epsom. The battalion had just had its commanding officer killed in Cheux and was to lose his replacement on the summit of Hill 112 two weeks later, when LtCol James was almost decapitated by German machine-gun fire. (IWM B6851)

Troops of 1st/7th Royal Warwickshire Regiment, 197th Brigade, 59th Staffordshire Division. The battalion is moving up towards Caen near St Contest on the second day of Operation Charnwood, 9 July. They are supported by Sherman tanks from 27th Armoured Brigade. (IWM 6758)

would not be allowed the luxury of concentrating their strength for a counterattack. With the enemy kept at arm's length by naval gunfire and continual fighter-bomber attacks, it would be the British Second Army that would gather its strength and threaten to break out towards Falaise, into the centre of France and the road to Paris. These moves would inevitably draw more and more enemy forces to the British sector.

While this was happening in the east of the landings, American First Army would consolidate its hold on the bridgehead in the west and then turn north with part of its forces to clear the Cotentin Peninsula and take Cherbourg. General Omar Bradley's First Army would then attack southwards, seize St Lô and concentrate its forces ready to fight a breakout battle. The breakthrough, when it came, would be exploited by General George S. Patton's US Third Army, which would by then be arriving in France. This was the crux of Allied strategy in Normandy: the British attacks would suck the main strength of the German forces in Normandy into the British sector. With the most powerful German units engaged in the struggle around Caen, the Americans could punch through to the west and break out into Brittany and south to the River Loire, hopefully against less formidable opposition.

In the event, things did not quite go according to plan, nor was this complete strategy quite as straightforward as outlined above. British 3rd Division was stopped short of Caen on D-Day and the Germans counterattacked with armour much earlier that the British thought possible. Further attempts by Second Army to take Caen with attacks by fresh formations to the east and west of the city also failed. Three weeks after D-Day an entire corps was given the task of sweeping round Caen from the west to get across the River Orne and onto the road network to the south, but the lead divisions never even made it to the river. Almost seven weeks after D-Day a powerful thrust by three armoured and two infantry divisions once again tried to get beyond Caen and onto the road to Falaise but failed with the loss of over 400 tanks. The Americans fared little better, confined as they were to fighting an infantryman's war in the claustrophobic countryside of the Normandy *bocage*. Fighting in

A Cromwell recovery tank from 11th Armoured Division hauling a damaged PzKpfw IV, which had been captured during the fighting near the River Odon. (IWM B6519)

terrain ideal for the German defenders, they were unable to make their numerical superiority in armour tell and their advance was painfully slow across fields and hedgerows and along sunken lanes riddled with German infantry and anti-tank weapons.

By the middle of July, the heavy losses suffered by the Allies and the hundreds of burnt-out British tanks that littered the battlefield around Caen, helped to convince Hitler that Normandy had to be the main Allied effort. Such losses could not be endured if the landings were just a diversion. The Führer finally began to release units from German Fifteenth Army and send them against the landings. The battle for Normandy degenerated into a giant slogging-match, with each side suffering horrendous casualties.

GERMAN PLANS

Before the invasion, Generalfeldmarschall Rommel, Commander of Army Group B, held Normandy with General Dollmann's Seventh Army. His divisions were strung along the coast protected by the steel and concrete fortifications of the Atlantic Wall. The wall had been strengthened and developed since Rommel had taken responsibility for it in late 1943, but it was still not as strong as Hitler and the German people were led to believe. The slaughter of Canadian 2nd Division and its immolation on the beaches during the August 1942 attack on Dieppe had convinced German High Command that strong coastal defences were the key to repelling any Allied invasion. The Canadians were unable to get off the beaches through the concentrated fire of relatively few well-sited weapons, housed in concrete pillboxes and on ground that commanded the shoreline. Hitler decided that an even greater concentration of fortifications should be built along the whole of the Channel coast to repel any further landings.

The purpose of the divisions manning the defences along the coast was to stall the invasion at the water's edge where it could be attacked by

Part of the great supply line that kept the tanks and vehicles in the frontline moving. Here 'jerrycans' are being filled by RASC personnel from a petrol lorry, which has brought the fuel forward from the petrol terminal. The petrol has been pumped over the Channel in an underwater pipeline from England (PLUTO). The petrol cans filled here will be loaded onto trucks that will take them up to the forward troops. (IWM B7734)

the Luftwaffe and the reserve units that would be rushed forward to seal off the landings. Rommel advocated keeping Panzer divisions close to the coast, within a day's march of possible landing sites. He stressed that the Allies would have to be swept back into the sea as they came ashore for the Germans to stand any chance of success. He knew the effectiveness of Allied air superiority and the difficulties of moving large bodies of troops over a road and rail system dominated by enemy fighter-bombers. He felt that if the Allies could get ashore and establish themselves, it would be impossible for the Germans to eject them subsequently.

Gerd von Rundstedt, C-in-C (West), and General Geyr von Schweppenburg, Commander of Panzer Group West, took an almost diametrically opposed view. Convinced that Allied air power and naval gunfire would undermine any German attempt to counter the landings near the coast, they both suggested the invasion should be attacked in strength by massed Panzer formations, at a point further inland and a time and place and on ground that was favourable to the German Army. The invasion was to be crushed in a decisive battle with such losses to the Allies that they would never try again.

Hitler vacillated between the two strategies, unable to choose between them and settled on a characteristically unsatisfactory fudge. He proposed that two armoured divisions be placed close to the northern coast of France under local control, while he withheld the remaining Panzer divisions until he had decided whether or not any landings were the main effort or just a diversion. This not only removed any prospect of the swift, decisive counterstroke favoured by Rommel, but also took effective operational control away from the commanders in the west and placed it in the capricious hands of the Führer himself.

Once the strategy of halting the invasion on the shoreline had failed on 6 June and the Allied beachhead was established, German options were greatly simplified. Clearly the invaders had to be pushed back into the sea. Although the concept was clear enough the execution proved difficult. Allied air superiority and the massive firepower of the fleet offshore, prevented the Germans from massing their strength for a

A Marder I, a 75mm Pak 40 (L/46) gun mounted on a captured French Hotchkiss H35 chassis, from 21st Panzer Division to the east of Caen. The division had 24 of these converted self-propelled guns. (Bundesarchiv 1011/493/3365/20)

decisive attack. The first two Panzer divisions to arrive in the area were committed to stopping the Allied advance on Caen. These units launched minor counterattacks trying to force a route through to the beaches, but each was beaten off without causing the British any great alarm, albeit with considerable casualties.

As the days and weeks went by, more and more German divisions, most of them armoured, made the painfully slow journey to Normandy. Hitler and Rommel always planned for an armoured thrust against the Allies and on paper it often appeared there were enough divisions in the line to do just that. In a situation that would become all too familiar in the last year of the war, however, the perception at OKW did not match the realities at the front. The relentless Allied pressure left the German forces constantly reacting to Montgomery's moves, repeatedly sending its powerful Panzer units to plug gaps in the line. This is not to suggest that the Germans danced entirely to Monty's tune; what strength they had and their tactical supremacy over the British allowed them to thwart most of Montgomery's meticulously organised plans. If the Germans had lost the initiative as a result of the pressure maintained through British superiority in numbers and in the air, Montgomery was unable to use this initiative to achieve anything close to a decisive result.

THE STRUGGLE FOR CAEN

D-DAY AND THE FIRST DRIVE FOR CAEN

Lieutenant-General Dempsey's British Second Army landed over 'Gold', 'Juno' and 'Sword' beaches on 6 June 1944 as part of the largest amphibious operation of the war. Lieutenant-General Crocker's I Corps landed Canadian 3rd Division (MajGen Keller) on 'Juno' Beach and British 3rd Division (MajGen Rennie) on 'Sword' Beach. Their task was to seize a beachhead and then move inland to secure the city of Caen and its bridges over the River Orne. The Canadians were to capture the airfield of Carpiquet and the high ground to the south-west of Caen while British 3rd Division drove straight inland to take the city. British XXX Corps (LtGen Bucknall) landed British 50th Division (MajGen Graham) on 'Gold' Beach with the tasks of linking up with the American landings on 'Omaha' Beach to the west, capturing the town of Bayeux and forming a solid centre to the Allied lodgement.

The landings themselves were a complete success. Allied forces broke through the defences of the Atlantic Wall in Normandy and formed a lodgement of sufficient strength to resist German attempts to destroy it. However, 3rd Division did not take Caen on D-Day, nor was the ground to the west of the city secured by the Canadians. The British advance stalled while still seven kilometres short of the city. The British had the misfortune to clash with 21st Panzer Division when the German armoured division pushed towards the sea around Lion sur Mer in an attempt to sweep the invaders from the beaches. After a promising start, Canadian 3rd Division also failed to reach their D-Day objectives.

The courtyard of Ardenne Abbey, advance headquarters of Kurt 'Panzer' Meyer's 25th SS-Panzergrenadier Regiment. It was through the archway in the corner that a total of 27 Canadian soldiers were taken on 8 and 9 June 1944 and executed with a pistol shot in the back of the head. After the war, Meyer was tried for these and other crimes and sentenced to death. The sentence was later commuted and he was released in 1954. (Ken Ford)

Alarmed by the German thrust down their left flank, the Canadians halted their advance and dug in to repel further attacks.

The two divisions of I Corps, together with their attendant armoured brigades, resumed the advance the next day. The British got no closer to Caen than they had the day before as they immediately clashed with the Panzergrenadiers of 21st Panzer Division who were dug in along the slope of hills to the north of Caen at Lébisey. A few more villages to the north-west of the city were occupied on 7 June, but when this advance was also met with a German counterattack, these troops also dug in and went onto the defensive. The division remained in these positions for the next four weeks.

When the Canadians resumed their advance the day after D-Day, they clashed with an advanced battlegroup of 12th SS-Panzer Division 'Hitlerjugend'. The SS unit had been ordered to the front late on 6 June along with the Panzer Lehr Division. During the night of 6/7 June, Standartenführer Kurt 'Panzer' Meyer, commander of 'Hitlerjugend's 25th SS-Panzergrenadier Regiment had moved the units that had arrived into the area around Ardenne Abbey a little to the west of Caen. He then prepared to launch a counterattack against the landings with Feuchtinger's 21st Panzer Division on the afternoon of 7 June. A little after midday Meyer saw the lead units of Canadian 3rd Division's 9th Brigade advancing straight across his front just over a kilometre from the abbey. Meyer waited for the right moment and then at 14.00hrs launched a perfect ambush against Canadian 9th Brigade and forced it to a halt with heavy losses in both infantry and tanks.

12th SS-Panzer Division launched further attacks against the Canadians over the next four days as the Germans attempted to effect a breakthrough to the sea, but each of them was repelled and the line held. The German division launched these attacks mostly in battalion strength, supported with only companies of tanks. Not once was 12th SS-Panzer Division assembled to make a powerful divisional thrust, aiming all of its undoubted might at just a narrow sector of the Canadian line where it could have easily

Canadian tanks and infantry of 3rd Division moving up from the beaches on the initial drive inland. (IWM B5388)

smashed its way through. It was compelled to use its force in 'penny packets' because of the lack of available infantry to hold the line (GenLt Richter's 716th Division, the only infantry in the area, had been effectively annihilated by the ferocity of the Allied landings). The SS Panzer division was forced onto the defensive as there were no other troops west of Caen capable of halting the Allied advance whilst it regrouped for a divisional attack. The German pressure did, however, also force the Canadians onto the defensive, halting them well short of their D-Day objectives. They too spent the next four weeks holding their position in the line.

To the west of 12th SS-Panzer Division, Panzer Lehr Division came into the line opposite British XXX Corps, facing 50th Northumbrian Division. Panzer Lehr was the strongest and best-equipped Panzer division in France and contained some of the most expert and experienced officers and NCOs in the German Army. With both the Panther medium tank and Tiger I heavy tank on its order of battle, it was a formidable outfit. Yet it too was forced onto the defensive and, far from concentrating for a powerful counterpunch, found itself holding a section of the line in an effort to halt the aggressive advance of 50th Division. The subsequent fighting was bitter, as XXX Corps attempted to push beyond the town of Tilly sur Seulles.

On the other side of the River Orne, British 6th Airborne Division had landed to the east of Caen during the early hours of 6 June. The airborne lodgement was connected to the Allied beachhead by a bridge over the River Orne at Bénouville and posed a serious threat to the enemy and his hold on Caen. Not surprisingly, the lightly-armed paratroopers were subjected to a series of attacks by enemy infantry and tanks. Each of them was beaten off with the help of artillery fire from the guns in I Corps' beachhead and by warships out at sea.

When the frontal assault failed to capture Caen, General Montgomery looked for another method to take the city and to establish his forces on the road network to the south. He proposed that XXX Corps sweep inland from the 'Gold' Beach bridgehead and then, with 7th Armoured Division, drive on Caen from the west. At the same time, 51st Highland Division would attack out of the airborne bridgehead east of the Orne.

COUNTERATTACK BY 12TH SS-PANZER DIVISION 'HITLERJUGEND'

7 June 1944, viewed from the south-east, showing the advance of Brigadier D.G. Cunnigham's Canadian 9th Infantry Brigade towards Carpiquet airfield and the explosive counterattack by a battlegroup from 12th SS-Panzer Division.

Note: Gridlines are shown at intervals of 1km/0.62 miles

ROSEL

736th
(elements)

KRUG

CHATEAU

GRUCHY

BAYEUX

AUTHIE

4

AIRFIELD

5

BUR

FRANQUEVILLE

10

6

9

11

4

CARPIQUET

ST CON

8

CUSSY

F

ARDENNE
ABBEY

7

G   B

A

C

25th SS

MEYER

ALLIED FORCES
Canadian 3rd Division
1   Canadian 9th Brigade
2   Stormont, Dundas and Glengarry Highlanders
3   North Nova Scotia Highlanders
4   Sherbrooke Fusiliers

9th Brigade, 3rd Division
5   1st King's Own Scottish Borderers
6   2nd Royal Ulster Rifles

GERMAN FORCES
12th SS-Panzer Division 'Hitlerjugend'
12th SS-Panzer Regiment
A   5th Company
B   6th Company
C   7th Company
D   8th Company

25th SS-Panzergrenadier Regiment
E   I Battalion
F   II Battalion
G   III Battalion

H   Elements of III/736th Regiment and
     Panzergrenadiers from 21st Panzer Division.

CAEN

12th SS

WITT

N

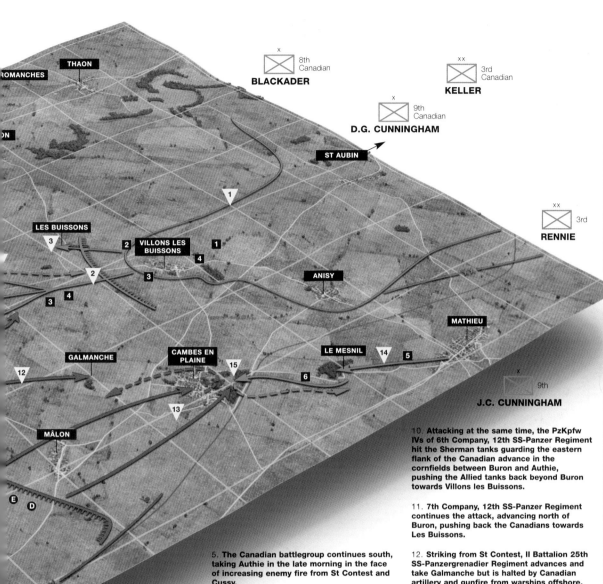

Map labels:

ROMANCHES
THAON
8th Canadian — **BLACKADER**
3rd Canadian — **KELLER**
9th Canadian — **D.G. CUNNINGHAM**
ST AUBIN
1
LES BUISSONS
3
VILLONS LES BUISSONS
2
1
4
2
3
4
3
3
ANISY
4
3rd — **RENNIE**
MATHIEU
GALMANCHE
12
CAMBES EN PLAINE
15
LE MESNIL
14
5
6
13
MÂLON
E
D
9th — **J.C. CUNNINGHAM**
21st — **FEUCHTINGER**

▼ EVENTS

1. Front line, Midnight, 6 June.

2. 07.45HRS, 7 JUNE. **A battlegroup of infantry from the North Nova Scotia Highlanders, riding in carriers, with Sherman tanks of the Sherbrooke Fusiliers advance south from Villons les Buissons towards Buron.**

3. The Stormont, Dundas and Glengarry Highlanders advance and take Les Buissons.

4. Canadian Infantry and tanks attack Buron, taking the village from isolated pockets of German 736th Regiment and a few elements of 21st Panzer Division. On either side of the village more Shermans swing wide of Buron and move south to give flank protection.

5. The Canadian battlegroup continues south, taking Authie in the late morning in the face of increasing enemy fire from St Contest and Cussy.

6. Leaving the infantry to dig in south of Authie, the Stuart light tanks of the Sherbrooke Fusiliers advance on Franqueville and are joined by a few Shermans that have swung wide of Authie.

7. Watching events unfold from a tower in the medieval Ardenne Abbey, Standartenführer Kurt Meyer cannot believe that a Canadian column is driving across the front of his 12th SS-Panzer Division battlegroup.

8. 14.00HRS, 7 JUNE. Meyer launches his counterattack, sending 5th Company, 12th SS-Panzer Regiment against the Canadian tanks in Franqueville. The PzKpfw IVs smash into the exposed flanks of the Sherbrooke Fusiliers and sweep them aside. The SS tanks then push northwards through the area of the Château on to Gruchy and Buron.

9. Behind a devastating barrage of artillery fire, German infantry from III Battalion, 25th SS-Panzergrenadier Regiment surprise the Canadians in Authie, annihilating virtually the whole of C Company of the Nova Scotias.

10. **Attacking at the same time, the PzKpfw IVs of 6th Company, 12th SS-Panzer Regiment hit the Sherman tanks guarding the eastern flank of the Canadian advance in the cornfields between Buron and Authie, pushing the Allied tanks back beyond Buron towards Villons les Buissons.**

11. 7th Company, 12th SS-Panzer Regiment continues the attack, advancing north of Buron, pushing back the Canadians towards Les Buissons.

12. Striking from St Contest, II Battalion 25th SS-Panzergrenadier Regiment advances and take Galmanche but is halted by Canadian artillery and gunfire from warships offshore.

13. The tanks of 8th Company, 12th SS-Panzer Regiment join with I Battalion, 25th SS-Panzergrenadier Regiment and attack Cambes en Plaine

14. **1st Kings Own Scottish Borderers, 9th Brigade, British 3rd Division move into Le Mesnil during the late afternoon.**

15. 18.00HRS, 7 JUNE. **2nd Royal Ulster Rifles attack Cambes and encounter Meyer's Panzergrenadiers and tanks in the village. Severe fighting forces 2nd Royal Ulster Rifles to retreat back to Le Mesnil. Under heavy artillery fire, 12th SS-Panzer Division 'Hitlerjugend' withdraws from Cambes to Galmanche, where it remains for the next month.**

16. Canadian 9th Brigade counterattacks to take Buron that evening, but is unable to hold any ground and all infantry and tanks are withdrawn back to a stop line running through Les Buissons, leaving the Germans in control of Buron and Authie, a position they will hold for the next four weeks.

The total dominance of the skies by the Allied air forces made all German movement during the day a most hazardous affair. Fighter-bombers would swoop out of the clouds and pounce on any enemy transport that could be found. As a result, almost all resupply of forward troops was done at night under the cover of darkness. (Bundesarchiv 1011/721/0363/34)

Montgomery had decided that the time was right to launch two veteran formations from his desert army against the Germans in France. When these divisions pushing either side of Caen had made sufficient progress, 1st Airborne Division would be dropped south of the city to link up with them and encircle Caen.

Air Chief Marshal Leigh Mallory, Commander-in-Chief Allied Expeditionary Air Force, immediately vetoed the plan, unhappy at parachute troops being used in this way. Montgomery decided to press on with the basic plan even without the paratroopers. The Highland Division began its attack south of Ranville on 11 June and attempted to take the village of Ste Honorine. They were repulsed by 21st Panzer Division with unexpectedly heavy losses. They tried again during the next two days but achieved few gains. It was great a disappointment to Montgomery; the famous Highlanders from the desert war appeared to have lost their cutting edge.

On 12 June over to the west of Caen, Monty's Desert Rats swung wide across the American sector and then through a gap in the German lines between Villers Bocage and Caumont. During the morning of 13 June the advance turned east and its leading units motored through the village of Villers Bocage. Then disaster struck. As the tanks and carriers of 4th County of London Yeomanry and 1st Rifle Brigade drove up the long slope away from the town a group of five PzKpfw VI Tiger Is opened fire on them. The unit of Tigers, 2. Kompanie schwere SS-Panzer-Abteilung 101, was commanded by the Panzer ace Hauptsturmführer Michael Wittmann and the young SS captain knocked out the leading carrier and blocked the road in front of the column. He then proceeded down the road towards Villers Bocage destroying each tank and vehicle he came across. The Cromwell tanks of 22nd Armoured Brigade fired furiously at the lumbering Tiger, but their 75mm shells bounced off its thick armour. Other Tigers from Wittmann's company joined in and in a matter of half an hour had blunted the advance of a whole British armoured division.

The camouflaged 'Operations Room' at Canadian 7th Brigade's HQ near Creully on 14 June. In the early days after the landings, advantage was taken of the fine weather and headquarters were often under canvas in wooded areas away from enemy observation and shellfire (Donald Grant, NAC PA 129041)

Those of the County of London Yeomanry that were able withdrew hurriedly back into the town and the accompanying infantry manoeuvred their anti-tank guns between buildings to try to halt the German attack. A Rifle Brigade anti-tank gun eventually immobilised Wittmann's tank and the crew escaped from the town on foot. The struggle continued for some time before the enemy withdrew, but it was enough to alarm the divisional commander MajGen Erskine. He ordered his advance brigade to withdraw and regroup and it was then hit by the newly arrived 2nd Panzer Division. Faced by such heavy resistance, the drive to outflank Caen from the west was called off and the Desert Rats withdrew back into XXX Corps' lodgement.

A Sherman tank dashes forward past a knocked-out PzKpfw IV near Cagny during the Goodwood battle in July. (IWM B7760)

The pierhead of the British Mulberry artificial harbour at Arromanches. The harbour was damaged in the storm that began on 19 June, but was soon back in service and remained in use for the rest of the war. (IWM A24371)

It became clear to Montgomery that the difficult Normandy *bocage*, which was characterised by networks of small fields surrounded by extremely substantial hedgerows with sunken lanes running between, was practically ideal ground for any force to defend. The hedgerows could easily conceal even the larger German anti-tank guns and German infantry armed with the highly effective Panzerfaust anti-tank rocket could remain concealed until a target was at point-blank range. All these factors combined to make it a nightmare arena for tanks. Supported by the Panzer forces now arriving at the front, it took only a few determined defenders to present any future British attack with a formidable obstacle.

Montgomery decided that it would require a military sledgehammer to overcome these obstacles – the next offensive would be a big one. He would launch completely fresh units untried in battle, consisting of two infantry divisions, one armoured division and two independent armoured brigades, against a narrow front and bludgeon his way through the German line. The main effort was again to be to the west of Caen and it would unleash 60,000 men, 600 tanks and 300 guns on the enemy. Before the commander of 21st Army Group could assemble this force, however, the weather turned against him.

The weather was always one of the few factors that the Allies had no control over, although they were aware of the potential trouble it could cause. If anything, Hitler depended on it. He knew that the uncertain nature of the English Channel, with its sudden squalls and prolonged periods of high winds, would eventually hit any Allied invasion. He always trusted that a summer storm striking the southern shore of the Channel would leave chaos in its wake. The Allies would need sheltered harbours through which to bring supplies and Hitler's strategy was built around the determination to deny them access to such a port. The Channel ports were heavily defended and the Führer made it clear to his commanders that their docks and facilities were to be destroyed should they be threatened with capture. The Allies anticipated that the Germans would seek to deny the ports to them and so developed prefabricated ports, called Mulberry harbours, which they could tow across the Channel and establish off the beaches of Normandy. Two were built: one for the Americans and one for the British.

A Forward Observation Officer and his orderly in the front line observing fire from the cruiser HMS *Exeter*. The orderly is passing back corrections to a naval wireless post that will relay the information to the warship offshore. (IWM B6630)

On 19 June, just as the last sections of these two great artificial harbours were being put into place, a great summer storm, even stronger than Hitler had hoped for, hit the Normandy coast. The American Mulberry off 'Omaha Beach' was almost destroyed, while the British port at Arromanches suffered extensive damage. The storm raged for four days completely disrupting the unloading and disembarkation of men and equipment. It was a great blow to Montgomery, as his divisions in the line needed a constant flow of stores and the storm disrupted that flow. His new divisions arriving from England spent days at sea waiting for the storm to abate. Montgomery had hoped to launch his new offensive on 21 June, but the storm meant this had to be postponed for five days. Five days without fresh supplies, five days of heavy rain and five days without air cover. The latter in particular was a great comfort to the enemy; for the first time since D-Day he could bring his forces forward in daylight, safe from the attentions of roaming Allied fighter-bombers.

It is interesting to note that the Americans, unlike the British, never attempted to rebuild their Mulberry harbour, having only agreed to have one in the first place to please the British Prime Minister, Winston Churchill, who was Mulberry's greatest advocate. They continued to use the straightforward method of landing supplies over open beaches after discovering that even relatively large vessels, especially LCTs (Landing Craft Tank) and LSTs (Landing Ship Tank) could be beached on the soft sand quite safely, unloaded and then refloated on the next tide. A tank landing ship Mark II could carry 300 troops and up to 60 tanks and vehicles right onto the beach. Other supplies could be ferried ashore using amphibious lorries (DUKWs) and large floating rafts (Rhinos). In the weeks after the storm, the Americans were to achieve daily deliveries of supplies that exceeded those landed through the British Mulberry harbour. In the week ending 29 June, the British landed 11,000 tons through the artificial port, while the Americans brought ashore 20,500 tons over the sands of 'Utah' and 'Omaha' beaches.

OPERATION EPSOM

By the last week in June, British XXX Corps had been in constant action since it had landed in France on D-Day, holding the western side of Second Army's lodgement. On the eastern side, British I Corps remained more or less in the positions it had achieved during the first few days of the landings, with the exception of 51st Highland Division, which had recently been in action in the airborne bridgehead on the other side of the River Orne. Between these two corps, Montgomery now inserted a new corps freshly arrived from England with a mind to use it in his latest offensive to encircle Caen – Operation Epsom.

Lieutenant-General Richard O'Connor began landing his VIII Corps just as the great storm hit the Normandy coast on 19 June. The resulting damage and disruption delayed the assembly of O'Connor's forces and brought about a short postponement to the start date of Epsom. The VIII Corps originally consisted of three new divisions: two infantry and one armoured, all untried in battle; a fourth division, 53rd Welsh Division, arrived in Normandy and joined the corps during the battle. The 11th Armoured Division was commanded by MajGen G.P.B. 'Pip' Roberts, 15th

LEFT **Troops from I Corps relaxing alongside the giant Anton-type bunker, which contained the plotting tables for the Luftwaffe radar station at Douvres and had been christened 'Hindenburg' by its previous occupants. (IWM B6307)**

BELOW **The hot dusty June weather made vehicle movement dangerous. The clouds of dust stirred up by transport attracted German gunfire. This sign near Cheux implores drivers to proceed with great caution. The 158 unit serial number and the Second Army tactical badge show that the vehicle belongs to 153rd RAC, of 34th Army Tank Brigade. (IWM B7018)**

An American-made 155mm 'Long Tom' gun in British service, firing at enemy concentrations in support of the infantry in early July. This gun is from one of Second Army's heavy artillery regiments in 4th Army Group Royal Artillery (4AGRA). (IWM B7005)

Scottish Division by MajGen G.H.A. MacMillan and 43rd Wessex Division was under the command of MajGen G. I. Thomas. Added to the corps for the battle, to give extra mobile punch and to exploit the breakthrough across the Orne, were the veteran 4th Armoured Brigade (Brig Currie) and the untried 31st Tank Brigade (Brig Knight), bringing up the number of tanks available for the operation to over 600.

Operation Epsom planned for VIII Corps to attack southwards out of the positions held by Canadian 3rd Division between Brouay and Bretteville L'Orgueilleuse, force crossings over the Odon and Orne rivers and then establish itself on the high ground north-east of Bretteville sur Laize to command the roads converging on Caen from the south. This would give Allied troops and tanks access to the Falaise plain south-east of the city. To protect VIII Corps' flanks, XXX Corps would attack alongside it to the west and secure the line Juvigny–Vendes–Rauray the day before the start of the operation. As the main attack progressed, I Corps would apply pressure on the enemy further east by sending Canadian 3rd Division against Carpiquet and its airfield, which remained uncaptured. Operation Epsom's start date was set for 26 June.

The VIII Corps' battle would begin with 15th Scottish Division attacking out of the front held by the Canadians towards the River Odon. The infantry, supported by the guns of I and XXX Corps as well as its own Corps artillery, would punch through the German defences to their front, which had been static since around 12 June. As the division pushed on to the River Odon, 43rd Wessex Division would follow behind mopping up enemy stragglers and securing those villages overrun by 15th Division. Once the Odon had been reached, 11th Armoured Division would cross the river and move onto the long ridge around Hill 112 and then advance down to the River Orne. The Scottish Division would then come forward, make an assault crossing of the river, allowing 11th Armoured Division to push on to the high ground overlooking the Caen–Falaise road.

Opposite VIII Corps in the line were the two German armoured divisions that had held the sector since 8 June. O'Connor's attack would hit the right of the Panzer Lehr Division and the left of 12th SS-Panzer Division 'Hitlerjugend'. Panzer Lehr was commanded by GenMaj Hyazinth von Gross-Zauche und Camminetz, Graf Strachwitz who had

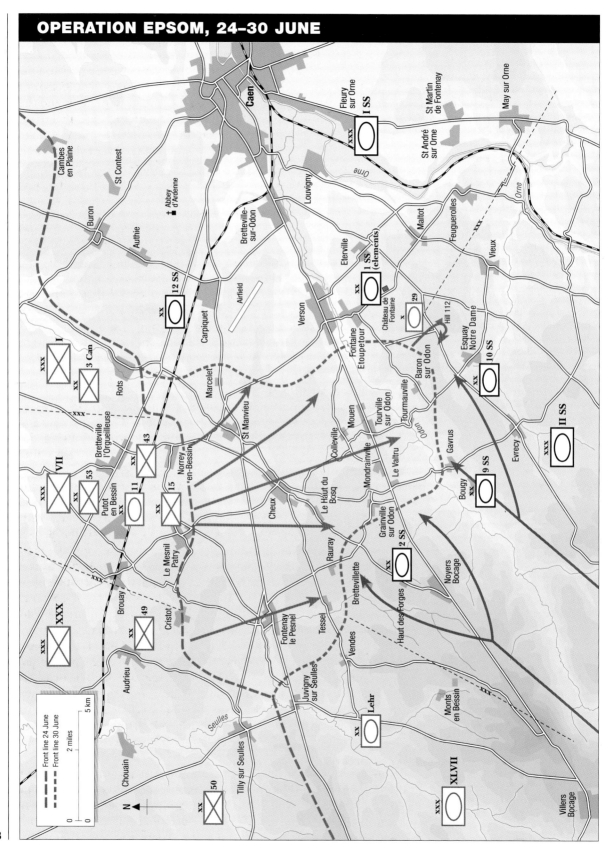

This 66ft-high observation tower was erected on high ground north of Cheux by VIII Corps Royal Engineers for 10th Survey Regiment Royal Artillery. Its observers were attempting to spot the flash of enemy guns near Verson and Hill 112 so that they could be targeted with counter-battery fire. (IWM B7043)

taken over command of the division on 8 June from GenLt Fritz Bayerlein, a veteran of the North African campaign where he had been Rommel's Chief of Staff. Oberführer Kurt Meyer now commanded 12th SS-Panzer Division following the death of its previous commander, Fritz Witt, killed by Allied shellfire on 14 June. Before joining 12th SS-Panzer Division, Meyer had served with the 1st SS-Panzer Division 'Leibstandarte SS Adolf Hitler' throughout Europe, earning himself the nickname 'Panzer' Meyer. Both of these armoured divisions had had ample time to establish formidable field defences to a depth of several kilometres. Adding firepower to the Panzer forces were almost 80 of the lethal 88mm guns from III Flak Corps. Although strictly anti-aircraft guns these weapons excelled in the anti-tank role.

The storm that had delayed the arrival of VIII Corps had also largely grounded Allied air power. This gave the enemy some respite from continual fighter-bomber attacks, which allowed him to bring more of his armoured forces forward into the battle area unmolested. By the time O'Connor was in position to launch his attack, several new German formations had moved into the area opposite Second Army. Rommel was gathering a powerful armoured force in preparation for a massive thrust against the Allied lodgement, manoeuvring it into position near to the junction of US First and British Second Armies. Both sides were readying themselves for the offensive. It was the British who struck first.

The Scottish Corridor

Operation Epsom, General Montgomery's third attempt to envelop Caen, did not get off to a good start. On 25 June, XXX Corps' opening moves against Rauray, to capture the higher ground overlooking the right flank of VIII Corps' advance, made slow progress. In its first battle the fresh British 49th Division was given the initial task of seizing Fontenay le Pesnil, then pushing on to Rauray and the high ground beyond. By the end of the day it had still not secured its first objective. Opposing the division were the Panzergrenadiers of Meyer's 12th SS-Panzer Division. Backed by tanks, the SS troops resisted the British attack with determination. Also involved in the struggle were the men of the Panzer Lehr Division who were drawn into the battle as the 49th Division hit their right flank on the ground to the north of Vendes. When Operation Epsom began the next day the hills along the Rauray spur, overlooking the ground over which the Scottish Division would advance, were still firmly in enemy hands and lined with tanks and guns.

The main thrust of Operation Epsom began at 07.00hrs on 26 June with a devastating barrage from the 700 guns of I, VIII and XXX Corps' artillery, supported by the 6in. guns of three cruisers and the 15in. weapons of the monitor *Roberts* anchored off the beaches. Bad flying-weather grounded air support from England, but 83 Group was able to fly its aircraft from their local airfields in Normandy. The group flew over 500 sorties during the day, but their efforts were hampered by low cloud and heavy ground mist.

At 07.30hrs, the 15th Scottish Division began its attack supported by 31st Tank Brigade, with 44th Lowland Brigade on the left and 46th Highland Brigade on the right. They set off on a 4km (2.46 miles) frontage behind a slow-moving barrage of shellfire that pounded the enemy in front of them. To begin with, progress was good and the

Scottish infantry moved out across open cornfields in good order, their front swept by plunging shellfire. When the Scotsmen began to reach the fortified villages in front of them, the advance slowed down alarmingly. The hamlet of La Guale was taken after a brief struggle, but St Manvieu, Cheux and Le Haut du Bosq were only partly occupied after hours of bitter hand-to-hand fighting. The 15th Division had found that the front line was only lightly held and that the main German line of defence was much further back. The artillery barrage had rolled over the Germans, causing only minor damage to those troops who were dug into well-constructed underground positions. Once the waves of shellfire had passed over them, the Panzergrenadiers emerged from their trenches and shelters to engage the Scottish troops at close quarters, often from their rear.

Fighting for control of the villages went on all morning. Once St Manvieu was finally taken, the Germans rapidly launched two counterattacks, first with tanks and infantry from 12th SS-Panzer Division then with a company of PzKpfw IVs from 21st Panzer Division who were holding the line to the left of 'Hitlerjugend'. Both attacks were beaten off by intense artillery fire. The long straggling village of Cheux was not fully occupied by the Glasgow Highlanders of 46th Brigade until late in the day. The battle to secure it had been bloody, with the battalion losing almost 200 men during this its first day of action. Cheux was now pounded by the German artillery situated on the high ground overlooking the village east of Rauray, still unaffected by 49th Division's attack that had started the day before. By the time 46th Brigade had established itself in Cheux, the village had been reduced to nothing more than piles of rubble and its roads were choked with collapsed buildings.

Two roads led south from Cheux towards the River Odon. One, to the south-west, passed through the eastern side of Le Haut de Bosq, through Grainville and Le Valtru on to the two bridges over the Odon at Gavrus. The other road led south-east towards Colleville, through Tourville to the bridge at Tourmauville. Lieutenant-General O'Connor now released

Infantry of 44th Brigade, 15th Scottish Division, advancing in open order through the wheat fields towards St Manvieu on the first day of 'Epsom'. (IWM B6618)

MajGen Roberts' 11th Armoured Division into the battle with orders to send its tanks along these two roads and seize the crossings over the Odon.

The armoured attack was slow in starting and its progress disappointing. The congested ruins of Cheux, under continuous shellfire from the enemy, delayed the deployment of 29th Armoured Brigade. When its tanks had finally picked their way through the battered ruins of Cheux and moved out to the south of the village, they were met by determined resistance and forced to a halt. Opposition from small groups of enemy infantry with well-concealed anti-tank guns picked off the Shermans, whilst longer range fire from 88mm guns on the high ground disrupted the advance. After two years of training as a composite armoured division with one tank brigade and one infantry brigade practising close armour/infantry co-operation, O'Connor chose to send 29th Armoured Brigade into its first battle without the supporting infantry of the division's 159th Brigade. It soon became clear that the tanks were not going to make the dash for the Odon before nightfall and at 18.00hrs the corps commander ordered the 15th Scottish Division to send its reserve brigade, 227th Infantry Brigade, forward to carry on the advance.

The third of the Scottish Division's brigades now went into action in pouring rain and met with the same ferocious opposition that had confronted 29th Armoured Brigade. On the right, progress along the road leading south-westwards was halted on the outskirts of Le Haut du Bosq by the guns positioned on the rising ground in front of Grainville. Fading light and driving rain helped confuse the advance and the infantry were quickly embroiled in close-quarters fighting and disjointed actions with enemy tanks. Continuous German mortaring broke up each of the Scottish attacks as it went in and the tank support fell victim to anti-tank gunfire. The advance along the road to Colleville fared only slightly better. An advance guard made it into the village, but the main body was held up along the diminutive Salbey stream about a kilometre south of Cheux. By the end of the day, the advance had stopped and the infantry were digging in for the night.

The first day of Operation Epsom had not been the hoped-for success. The Odon had not been reached and the high ground barring the way

A burning Panther tank in an orchard in Cheux, knocked out during an enemy counterattack against 15th Scottish Division during Operation Epsom. (IWM B6055)

Infantry crawling through high standing corn. The wide wheatfields were devoid of any cover and infantry advancing across them were easy targets for enemy machine-gunners. The troops found it was much safer to go to ground and edge their way forwards. It made for slow progress, but they were at least out of the enemy's sight while they did so. (IWM B6756)

Sherman Firefly tank, fitted with the powerful 17-pdr gun. The Sherman had an unenviable reputation for vulnerability and a strong tendency to burst into flames when hit. Its normal main armament was a 75mm, which was not capable of inflicting any serious damage on the enemy's more heavily-armoured Tiger and Panther tanks. A number were produced with the British 17-pdr anti-tank gun, which packed a punch capable of knocking out the heavy German tanks. In armoured units there was one Firefly per troop of four tanks. (IWM B5546)

south was still in enemy hands. XXX Corps' progress to the west had been equally unimpressive, with Rauray and its spur still in enemy hands. On a positive note the two German divisions opposing the attack had been forced to employ their last reserves of men and tanks, had suffered considerable losses, and had not been able to mount any effective counterattacks. General Dollmann of German Seventh Army saw the containment of the British offensive as an outright defensive victory. He now ordered 1st SS-Panzer Division to move against the eastern sector of the British penetration when it had completed its transit from Belgium. Dollmann also knew that II SS-Panzer Corps would soon be arriving in the sector after its long trek from Russia. The next day he might well be ready to launch his major armoured attack against the Allies.

'Ultra' intercepts had informed Montgomery of these moves. He knew that the elite 1st SS-Panzer Division 'Leibstandarte' was on its way from Belgium and that Obergruppenführer Bittrich's II SS-Panzer Corps, including 9th and 10th SS-Panzer Divisions, was in transit to Normandy

The bridge over the River Odon at Tourmauville captured by 15th Scottish Division in the Epsom offensive. During the operation, this was the only crossing place available over which tanks and vehicles could get into VIII Corps' bridgehead beneath Hill 112. (Ken Ford)

from the east. The RAF now stepped up its interdictory raids on these units and attacked them mercilessly with its fighter-bombers during their passage. Key railway targets in France and Belgium were again bombed by heavy and medium bombers to disrupt all troop movements, forcing many of the SS Panzergrenadiers to detrain and march into Normandy by road from south of Paris.

Operation Epsom continued on 27 June with 15th Division once more entering the attack at 05.00hrs. The 43rd Wessex Division had come forward to take over the captured villages and allow the Scottish Division to continue the advance to the Odon. However, the further 15th Division and 11th Armoured Division pushed forwards, the greater was the salient being carved out of enemy territory and the longer their exposed flanks became. More and more of the tanks and infantry of VIII Corps had to be employed holding these gains, rather than securing additional ground. The Sherman tanks of 4th Armoured Brigade and the heavy Churchills of 31st Tank Brigade were now deployed east and west of the main attack to hold the flanks of the salient.

Epsom had now become a slogging-match, a war of attrition to break the enemy. Once again heavy fighting on the western road south of Cheux limited the move towards Grainville and the Scotsmen of 15th Division battered away all day against determined enemy resistance, without getting past Le Haut du Bosq. On the road from Cheux to the south-east, determined infantry attacks took Colleville and then pushed on to take Tourville and Mondrainville. 15th Scottish Division was now looking down into the valley of the River Odon.

In mid afternoon, 2nd Argyll and Sutherland Highlanders from 227th Brigade came forward and pushed down the slopes to the river, seizing the bridge over the Odon at Tourmauville and establishing a bridgehead on the far side. This was immediately exploited by 23rd Hussars from 11th Armoured Division, who crossed the bridge and moved out southwards onto the long northern slopes of Hill 112. With tanks over the river guarding the lodgement, it was time to bring forward the division's other two armoured battalions and infantry. The Shermans of 2nd Fife and Forfar Yeomanry and 3rd Royal Tank Regiment now prepared to join the Hussars across the Odon. They would be followed by the 3rd Monmouthshires and 4th King's Shropshire Light Infantry from 159th Brigade who were to occupy the villages of Baron and Tourmauville respectively.

The 15th Division was now positioned on the Caen–Villers Bocage road and was able to send a battalion westwards in an attempt to force its way into Grainville from the east and relieve the bottleneck on the road south-west from Cheux. This was no easy task as the SS troops defending Grainville were determined to hold onto the village. Although the Scotsmen finally fought their way to the outskirts of Grainville, it was too late to capture the place before nightfall.

The second day of Epsom had finished with moderate gains, but had not achieved a major breakthrough. XXX Corps had at last captured Rauray, but the high ground overlooking O'Connor's advance was still in enemy hands. VIII Corps had driven a corridor into the enemy lines 4km wide and 8km deep, but the spearhead of this thrust was still being blunted by crack enemy formations. On a positive note, the River Odon had been reached and crossed, but the bridgehead across it was being supplied along just one road and maintained over just the lone bridge at Tourmauville. The second column moving south through Grainville was still stalled near Le Haut de Bosq. The operation was also absorbing most of VIII Corps' assets at an early stage; LtGen O'Connor had fed 43rd Division into the salient and deployed his two independent armoured brigades just to hold the flanks. Enemy activity on these flanks was causing concern; several determined counterattacks by SS Panzergrenadiers backed by tanks were making the whole salient look vulnerable. A company of Panther tanks had actually penetrated right into Cheux and was only beaten off with considerable losses on both sides. These losses to 12th SS-Panzer Division were made good with the addition of a battalion of tanks from 2nd Panzer Division and a Tiger battalion from I SS-Panzer Corps.

The third day of Operation Epsom, 28 June, was again gloomy and overcast, limiting the air support available from England. South of the Odon at Tourmauville, 11th Armoured Division strengthened and enlarged the bridgehead with 29th Armoured Brigade pushing its tanks out onto the open cornfields covering the slopes of Hill 112. The enemy had had ample time to arrange his defences around this strategically important high ground and he met the advance with tanks, anti-tank guns and mortars. Fire hit the Shermans of 11th Armoured Division from three sides. Ahead of them was the round summit of Hill 112, lined with carefully concealed anti-tank guns. To the right, more high ground held German artillery batteries that plastered the open fields with explosives, and to the left rear, in the wooded valley behind Baron, more guns poured down shell and mortar fire. The fighting and manoeuvring that criss-crossed the bare sides of the hill went on all morning. At around midday the armoured division pulled back its tanks into the bridgehead occupied by its infantry and repelled several German counterattacks. Major-General Roberts was told to hold his advance until 15th Scottish and 43rd Wessex Divisions had cleared the western ground between Cheux and the Odon and established more crossings over the river.

A dead German SS Panzer-grenadier wearing the camouflage smock favoured by SS troops. His pockets have clearly been checked for anything useful and his boots have also been removed. The SS units bitterly resisted Montgomery's attempts to capture Caen but paid a high price in casualties. (Ken Bell, NAC PA 132191)

Meanwhile, 15th Division was slogging away south of Cheux. Two battalions of infantry supported by tanks were sent to clear the ground to the west of the road to Grainville and the Rauray spur to allow the advance southwards to continue. Strong enemy opposition frustrated the move, but troops did manage to get into Grainville later that day linking up with the troops advancing westwards from Colleville. These moves allowed the capture of Mondrainville and Le Valtru, but the enemy resolutely refused to give up the ground between Le Valtru and the Odon.

On the other side of the River Odon, 2nd Argyll and Sutherland Highlanders had been busy. After capturing the Tourmauville bridge the day before, they had pushed along the southern bank of the river and captured the village of Gavrus and its two bridges over the Odon. Unfortunately, the remainder of the division remained stalled between Le Valtru and the Gavrus bridges. This left the Argylls completely isolated, holding bridges south of the Odon that could not be used from the north.

This third day of battle had seen little increase on the gains made on the first two days, but at least the ground won by VIII Corps was now more firmly held. This proved to be most important, as enemy prisoners captured along the flanks of the salient came from German units new to the sector. These prisoners included men from 2nd Panzer and 1st and 2nd SS-Panzer Divisions. They confirmed that 1st SS-Panzer Division 'Leibstandarte' was in the latter stages of completing its move from Bruges and that 2nd SS-Panzer Division had finished its long trek up through France from Toulouse, having left a trail of atrocities and massacres in its wake, most notably at Tulle and Oradour sur Glane. There was also evidence that II SS-Panzer Corps had arrived in Normandy, bringing 9th and 10th SS-Panzer Divisions into the line. It seemed that Operation Epsom was attracting all the enemy Panzer divisions into British Second Army's sector. It was convincing evidence that Rommel was preparing to launch a major counterattack against the invasion. With the danger of this imminent attack, LtGen O'Connor decided not to continue his advance any further southwards towards the River Orne until the position north of the Odon was made more secure.

The flanks of the penetration had to be strong enough to repel the German attack when it came.

The fourth day of the battle, 29 June, was spent bringing more infantry forward to hold important pressure points and to push the enemy back from the shoulders of the salient. The 129th Brigade from 43rd Division took Mouen and cleared the wooded area along the Odon to the east of Baron. In the west of the corridor, 15th Scottish tried to extend their ground towards the road from Noyers to Cheux that led through Le Haut de Bosq. In this they were unsuccessful, as the enemy was determined to retain the high ground between Noyers and Brettevillette. This high ground gave the Germans a dominant view of the battlefield and would be one of the bases from which to launch their counterattack. South of the Odon, 11th Armoured Div. had extended its bridgehead around Baron and reached the road that crosses Hill 112 at Esquay, sending one company of infantry up into the wood on top of the hill.

On 29 June the weather cleared to a perfect summer's day and the RAF took great advantage to resume its domination of the skies over Normandy. Second Tactical Air Force was out in strength throughout the day responding to air reconnaissance reports of large-scale enemy troop movements towards the battlefield. All approaches to the sector were attacked by fighter-bombers and rocket-firing Typhoons. Any enemy movement along roads in their rear was pounced on, as were known German headquarters and assembly areas. This deluge of bombing and strafing was supplemented by long-range artillery fire and naval gunfire from warships off the coast. It seemed that any and every enemy troop concentration was being pounded before it could reach the battlefield. One possible enemy attack, including over 40 tanks, that was being assembled to the east of the Scottish salient near Carpiquet, was so heavily attacked that nothing more was seen or heard of the battlegroup that day.

Memorial to 15th Scottish Division by the side of the road that leads down to the Tourmauville bridge over the Odon. (Ken Ford)

German command bunker near the present-day passenger terminal at Carpiquet airfield. Many of the concrete fortifications around the airfield had been constructed before the invasion and were strengthened after the landings to help defend Caen. The presence of these impregnable positions garrisoned by 12th-SS Panzer Division made Carpiquet and its airfield a formidable obstacle for the Canadians. (Ken Ford)

British troops dug in on the edge of a field overlooking Hill 112. This scene perfectly captures the lot of the common soldier in wartime – 99 per cent boredom, 1 per cent terror. (IWM B7441)

The German Counterattack

Even with such a high level of interdictory fire, the enemy still managed to assemble his forces in strength for the planned counterattacks. The first of these hit 44th Brigade of the Scottish Division along the Noyers–Cheux road at about 18.00hrs. Three battalions of German infantry supported by tanks from 9th SS-Panzer Division struck the Scottish troops. At first the line held, but constant pressure began to force the Lowland Brigade back. The balance was redressed by the arrival of tanks from 4th Armoured Brigade and by the self-propelled guns of VIII Corps' tank-buster regiment, 91st Anti-tank Regiment, Royal Artillery, which were lined up in depth behind the infantry. With the Scots troops keeping the enemy infantry at bay, the enemy tanks were destroyed in detail as they tried to penetrate the defensive line. By nightfall the line was stabilised, contact with 49th Division established, and the enemy attack blunted.

The next German attack was against 46th Highland Brigade holding the villages of Grainville, Mondrainville and Le Valtru. It began with heavy artillery fire and enemy infantry trying to infiltrate between the villages. Then came the tanks, including some flame-throwers. Fighting was fierce as the enemy penetrated the brigade's positions especially around Le Valtru. During the evening MajGen MacMillan committed his two reserve battalions from 227th Brigade to reinforce the villages and sought help from 31st Tank Brigade, who responded with the heavy Churchills of 7th Royal Tank Regiment. The battle continued well into the night before the position along the north bank of the Odon was stabilised. Once again, determined resistance and overwhelming artillery fire was too much for the enemy. The Germans broke off the attack.

Contemporaneously with these two enemy counterattacks, 9th SS-Panzer Division 'Hohenstaufen' and elements of 2nd SS-Panzer Division 'Das Reich' also struck south of the Odon. A battlegroup of infantry and tanks hit the exposed 2nd Argylls in Gavrus. For the next 5¹/₂ hours the vulnerable Scottish battalion held on to its precarious bridgehead. The enemy pressed hard and the perimeter around the bridges shrank alarmingly, but the Scotsmen held on. At around 20.30hrs the Germans withdrew.

The enemy also hit 11th Armoured Division and 4th Armoured Brigade on Hill 112. Panzers and Panzer-grenadiers, supported by self-propelled guns from 10th SS-Panzer Division 'Frundsberg', attacked along the ridge from the west. 44th Royal Tank Regiment lost six of its tanks in quick succession and the armoured line swung back in the face of the enemy onslaught. In the valley nearer the river, German groups penetrated through to the line held by the infantry of 159th Brigade near Baron. The division's Sherman tanks, spread out across Hill 112, now became vulnerable to the enemy infantry arriving in their rear. The strength and ferocity of these enemy counterattacks were beginning to alarm Dempsey at Second Army HQ.

A chaplain gives absolution to a dying Canadian soldier during the attack on Caen in July. (Harold G. Aikman, NAC PA 136042)

Intelligence reports demonstrated that the enemy was still massing his Panzer divisions for a concerted armoured strike against the salient. The attacks of 29 June were seen as preliminary moves before the big offensive. The British armour to the south of the Odon now looked weak and it was in the wrong place to be able to react to any German penetration in the north of the salient. At 22.00hrs, LtGen Dempsey ordered those tanks of 11th Armoured Division across the Odon to be withdrawn to the north bank and stationed in the rear ready to counter the expected German attack. 159th Infantry Brigade was to remain holding the bridgehead and come under command of 15th Scottish Division. 43rd Wessex Division was to take over the left of the corridor, while 15th Scottish Division concentrated its forces on the right. Second Army also released the 32nd Guards Infantry Brigade from the Guards Armoured Division to hold the northern part of the left flank of the corridor opposite Carpiquet.

Dempscy was convinced that the next German attack would be heavy and would constitute the main assault against ·the salient and the Allied lodgement in Normandy. During the night the tanks of 29th and 4th Armoured Brigades came down from their exposed positions around Hill 112 and withdrew into the relative safety of the Scottish corridor. This vitally important area of high ground was given back to the enemy without a fight, a decision that was to haunt Dempsey later when thousands of men fell trying to regain it during the July offensives.

On 30 June, VIII Corps braced itself to receive the German attack, but none came. There was some skirmishing along the line as both sides jockeyed for position, but the expected blow never fell. The next day the enemy did come at O'Connor's men, but not with the ferocity that was anticipated. British artillery and the RAF saw to it that every enemy concentration was targeted with heavy fire. During the early hours of 1 July, German units began to probe the line, attacking from the west along either side of the Odon. By 09.45hrs the enemy accepted that II SS-Panzer Corps had been stopped by heavy artillery concentrations.

He tried again in the early afternoon and once more in the evening, but made little headway against determined British opposition, leaving 40 tanks destroyed on the battlefield. The enemy had suffered a sharp defeat, but Dempsey was convinced that. with so many Panzer divisions in the area, a stronger attack was yet to come.

In the event Dempsey was too cautious. VIII Corps had blunted the main German effort and the British had forestalled the last major attempt to launch a massed armoured attack against the landings. The fresh Panzer divisions had been fed into the battle piecemeal, never allowed to concentrate for the planned big thrust. The other German armoured divisions already in the line had gradually been bled of their strength over the preceding weeks, having been used to plug gaps in the front. Epsom had failed to achieve almost any of its objectives, but it could be credited with frustrating German plans to push the Allies back into the sea.

OPERATION CHARNWOOD: THE CAPTURE OF CAEN

While the Epsom offensive was still at its height, both the C-in-C (West) and the commander of Army Group B visited Hitler at his retreat at Berchtesgaden. Von Rundstedt and Rommel both told the Führer that the position in Normandy was critical and that there should be some sort of a controlled withdrawal to a more easily defended line, out of range of the naval guns. Hitler told them he would consider the situation, but before they had even made the journey back to France, he sent an order that the present line must be defended at all costs.

When the news was given to Obergruppenführer Paul Hausser (temporarily commanding Seventh Army after the suicide on 29 June of Generaloberst Dollmann) and to General der Panzertruppen Geyr von Schweppenburg, commander of Panzer Group West, they both submitted reports advocating an immediate evacuation of Caen and a withdrawal to a new line. Rommel and Von Rundstedt both once again agreed and a forceful new report was sent to the High Command at OKW saying the line must be shortened and I and II SS-Panzer Corps pulled back to reserve to preserve their strength to fight a new battle on a tactically suitable line. Hitler was furious. On 2 July, he once more issued instructions that there would be no withdrawal and then dismissed Von Rundstedt, replacing him with Generalfeldmarschall von Kluge. The new C-in-C (West) arrived in Paris on the same day that Von Rundstedt left. Von Kluge was brimful of confidence regarding his ability to hold the Allies and proceeded to tell Rommel that he too would have to get accustomed to carrying out orders. On 4 July Hitler struck again, replacing Geyr von Schweppenburg with the veteran Panzer leader General der Panzertruppen Heinrich Eberbach as head of Panzer Group West.

The Canadians and Carpiquet Airfield
After Operation Epsom had ground to a halt in the face of enemy counterattacks, LtGen Dempsey switched his attention back to the thorny problem of Carpiquet airfield. The Canadians had been looking

down on the site since 7 June, but had not attacked the complex of hangars and buildings surrounding the landing ground, which the enemy held in strength. In the meantime, the Germans had reinforced their hold on the airfield, which had been in use by them since 1940. Even before the Canadians had arrived, pillboxes, wire and anti-aircraft positions protected the village of Carpiquet and its airfield. After D-Day the area had been further fortified and developed into a formidable strongpoint, upon which the defences of the western approaches to Caen were anchored. Its garrison consisted of units from 12th SS-Panzer Division, including 1st, 3rd and 4th Companies of 26th SS-Panzer-grenadier Regiment – a total of about 150 Panzergrenadiers. Approximately 50 were in the village, with the other 100 entrenched amongst the hangars and bunkers surrounding the airfield. The 9th Company of 12th SS-Panzer Regiment had five PzKpfw IVs covering the entire width of the landing ground. A battery of 88mm anti-aircraft guns from Flakabteilung 12, covered the area from positions to the north-east

Operation Windsor, the task of capturing Carpiquet village and the airfield, was once again given to Canadian 3rd Division, who had been expected to seize it on 7 June. The operation planned for Canadian 8th Brigade, comprising the North Shore Regiment, the Queen's Own Rifles of Canada and Le Régiment de la Chaudière, to attack from west to east out of ground held by 32nd Guards Brigade, starting from a secure base around the village of Marcelet. The brigade had a further battalion under command, the Royal Winnipeg Rifles, to help in the attack. At the same time, 214th Brigade from 43rd Wessex Division would protect the Canadian brigade's right flank by attacking south-east to occupy Verson and the area along the Odon that had not been secured during Operation Epsom. The brigade was also supported by the Sherman tanks of the Fort Garry Horse, a regiment of self-propelled tank destroyers, specialised tank support from 79th Armoured Division, a machine-gun battalion, 21 regiments of field artillery, the massive guns of the battleship HMS *Rodney* and the monitor *Roberts,* together with two squadrons of Typhoon rocket-firing aircraft. This represented a massive commitment of assets to capture an area of just over four square kilometres garrisoned by 150 Germans.

The attack began on 4 July with the guns of the *Rodney* firing 15 rounds from her 16in. guns at 24,000m (26,200yds) range against the buildings around Carpiquet. At 05.00hrs, behind a tremendous artillery barrage, three infantry battalions of Canadian 8th Brigade moved eastwards in the half-light of dawn towards the airfield and the village. A battalion of German artillery from 12th SS-Panzer Division located on the outskirts of Caen immediately replied with a counter-barrage, which caught the Canadian troops in their forming-up area. On the left, the Chaudières, North Shore Regiment and the Queen's Own Rifles gained Carpiquet village after a fierce struggle, but the Winnipeg Rifles could not get within striking distance of the hangars on the southern perimeter of the airfield and were beaten back with tremendous losses. All four Canadian battalions suffered considerably during the attacks. The Winnipeg Rifles tried again in the late afternoon, reaching the half-demolished hangars only to be driven out again later in the day by the five 'Hitlerjugend' PzKpfw IVs. The Winnipegs then fell back to their start line in Marcelet.

All that remained of the village at Carpiquet after the battle was this part of the doorway into the local church. It has now become a memorial to those who died during the fighting. (Ken Ford)

OPERATION CHARNWOOD AND THE CAPTURE OF CAEN

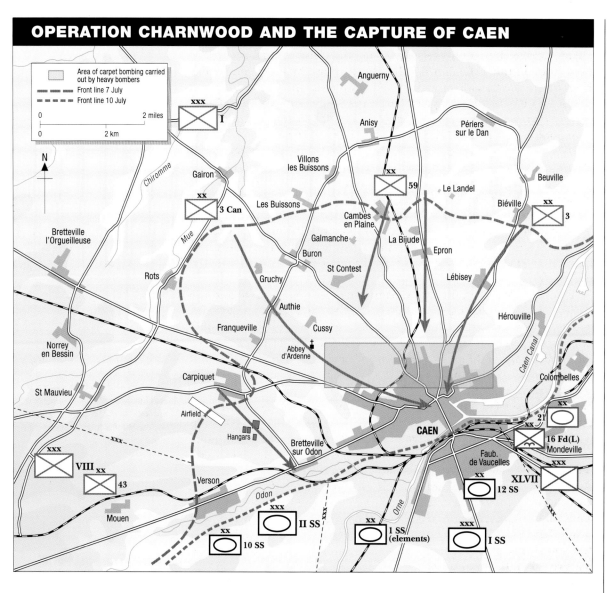

The Canadians in Carpiquet were counterattacked during the night by troops from III Battalion, 1st SS-Panzergrenadier Regiment, 1st SS-Panzer Division 'Leibstandarte SS Adolf Hitler'. The enemy came at the Chaudières from the north, from the direction of the village of Franqueville. This attack was used as a diversion to allow the 'Hitlerjugend' troops to withdraw from the buildings at the southern end of the airfield and move into the barracks and hangars on the eastern perimeter. The attack from the north was beaten off, but the withdrawal in the south was completed without loss. On 5 July, each side counted its losses and bombarded each other with artillery, whilst Typhoons from 83 Group strafed and rocketed the area. The Canadians suffered 377 casualties in their attack on Carpiquet, including 132 dead. The Germans suffered 32 killed and 48 wounded. Further operations to take the hangers and barracks on the eastern side of the airfield were postponed. British Second Army was about to launch a new attack against Caen that would bludgeon and bomb the city into submission. The capture of the remainder of the airfield could wait.

The Fall of Caen

General Montgomery had tired of trying to outflank Caen to the west, south and east. He now decided to take a rather more direct approach to the problem, hurling Second Army straight at the city in a massive display of brute force and overwhelming air power. British I Corps was once again given the opportunity of fulfilling its D-Day objective of seizing Caen and the bridges over the River Orne. With 115,000 men from three infantry divisions, supported by a range of other formations, LtGen Crocker's Corps was to attack straight down the roads from the north and smash its way through to the city centre and its bridges. Prior to their advance an immense air raid by the heavy bombers of RAF Bomber Command would pulverise the enemy in front of the attacking troops.

Since D-Day, the Germans had been fortifying the area to the north of Caen. Anti-tank ditches and weapons pits had been strengthened by the addition of minefields and other obstacles. A defensive belt between three and four kilometres deep had been constructed, with virtually every infantry position below ground. The ring of villages from Lébisey near the Orne Canal round to Franqueville near Carpiquet had been turned into tank-proof strongholds, able to support each other with interlocking fields of fire. Dug-in tanks, assault guns and multi-barrelled mortars were emplaced to support the infantry. Behind this defensive belt, more artillery and mortar positions covered the ground over which the British were to attack.

The German front line to the north of the city, from Hérouville to Cambes, was held by 16th Luftwaffe Field Division from LXXXVI Corps, with tanks from 21st Panzer Division in support – the bulk of the Panzergrenadiers from the depleted division were out of the line resting.

The burning centre of Caen taken before Operation Charnwood. Since D-Day the city had been bombed and shelled by the Allies. Most of the large-scale destruction caused by the heavy bombers during Charnwood was in the northern part of the city, but as the fighting moved through Caen towards the bridges over the Orne, the buildings around the river were also completely obliterated. The foreground shows the area just north of the Bassin St Pierre, visible on the left of the photo. The church steeple, just visible through the smoke in the background, is probably that of St Jean. (IWM CL3945)

A German PzKpfw IV tank dug into a hull-down position. The tank was part of the defences on the northern approach into Caen near Lébisey, along the axis attacked by British 3rd Division. This tank had a good field of fire and its low profile made it very difficult to spot and destroy. (IWM B7056)

From Cambes to Carpiquet airfield, the front was held by I SS-Panzer Corps with 12th SS-Panzer Division, 7th Werfer Brigade and detachments of Panzergrenadiers from 1st SS-Panzer Division – the remainder of 'Leibstandarte' was still completing its move from Belgium. Distributed around the Caen area, watching both the skies and the approaches to the city, were the dual-purpose 88mm guns of III Flak Corps.

The operation to capture Caen, codenamed 'Charnwood', was set to begin on the morning of 8 July. The night before, the RAF would bomb the area of Caen that lay in front of the attacking troops in an effort to clear the German defenders. It was the first occasion on which strategic bombers would be used in Normandy as tactical support for ground forces. To safeguard the leading formations of I Corps, it was decided that the bombline should be 6,000 metres ahead of the nearest troops. Although a prudent precaution – no one wanted British troops to be bombed by the RAF – the reality was that the forward edge of the German defences was just a few hundred metres from the British troops and to bomb a line 6,000 metres behind them was simply unloading high explosive on the rear area of the northern outskirts of the city mostly populated by French civilians. Tanks and infantry would have to advance six kilometres through the main belt of enemy fortifications before they reached the ground 'cleared' by the bombing.

The plan was for I Corps to attack Caen from the north using British 3rd Division, the newly arrived 59th Staffordshire Division and Canadian 3rd Division. The infantry would be supported by the specialised armour of 79th Armoured Division and the tanks of 27th and Canadian 2nd Armoured Brigades. Artillery support would be provided by the 25-pdr guns of the attacking infantry divisions, together with the artillery of the Guards Armoured Division and 51st Scottish Division. Heavier artillery fire was to come from 3rd and 4th Army Groups Royal Artillery and from warships out at sea. The cruisers, *Belfast* and *Emerald*, the monitor *Roberts* and the battleship *Rodney* would all bombard the enemy's positions with large calibre shells.

In the late afternoon of 7 July, the barrage began when the warships off the coast pounded known German strongpoints in Caen with shells from 6in. to 16in. in calibre. Later that evening, a steady stream of Lancaster and Halifax heavy bombers from the RAF laid a carpet of high explosive across

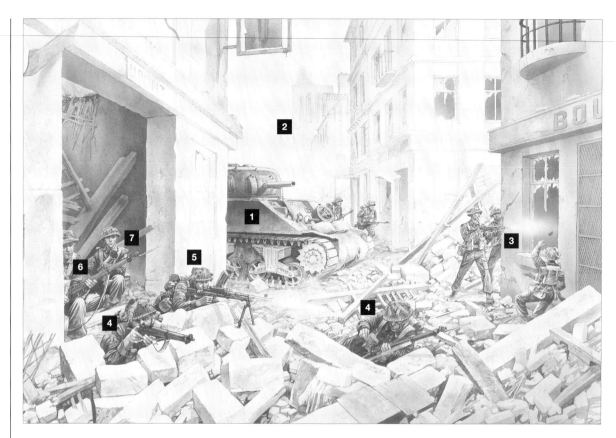

THE REGINA RIFLES STREETFIGHTING IN CAEN,
9 JULY 1944 (pages 54–55)

Operation Charnwood succeeded in getting British and Canadian troops and tanks into Caen and capturing that part of the city north of the River Orne, but at a heavy cost to the fabric of the town and to the lives of its citizens. Large areas of Caen were completely obliterated, razed to the ground by Allied bombers and shellfire. Across the northern suburbs, in front of the advance of British I Corps, a great swath of the city had been pounded to rubble. Close to the river around the important bridges across the Orne, similar tracts of the centre had been reduced to a chaotic jumble of broken masonry and stone. All over Caen stray bombs and shells had torn apart individual buildings on virtually every street. Canadian 3rd Division had to fight a particularly nasty battle on the western outskirts of Caen before it could enter the city. Determined set-piece infantry attacks were required to regain the ground it had given up over a month earlier to 12th SS-Panzer Division 'Hitlerjugend'. The Regina Rifles were given the task of taking Ardenne Abbey, the HQ of 'Panzer' Meyer's 25th SS-Panzergrenadier Regiment. A night attack supported by armour eventually got the battalion into the venerable abbey buildings, but with an alarming number of casualties. The SS troops had fought ferociously throughout the night, resisting the Canadians with great venom, then silently withdrew south-eastwards into Caen just as the abbey fell. Advance units of the Reginas followed on into the city from the west only to be embroiled in house-to house fighting. Allied progress into Caen was hampered by the widespread

destruction, and the infantry were forced to probe their way into the centre without the support of armour. As the second day of the operation wore on, bulldozers and engineers gradually cleared paths along certain thoroughfares, allowing Sherman tanks from Canadian 2nd Armoured Brigade (1) to push forward to support the leading troops. The Regina Rifles used the route from Bayeux as its axis of advance, which brought it into the city close to the Abbaye aux Hommes (2), the great medieval church that contained the tomb of William the Conqueror. Enemy resistance in the city was sporadic, with the bulk of the German defenders withdrawing across the river whilst an escape route remained open. Behind them, a rearguard sniped and harassed the British and Canadian infantry as they advanced cautiously through the broken streets. One enemy sniper or a small group of enemy troops could bring the advance to a halt and then melt away into the next bombed-out shell of a building to stall the advance once more as it resumed. Each house had to be systematically cleared room by room with small arms and grenades (3). Here men of the Regina Rifles deal with a pocket of enemy resistance. Members of the platoon suppress the enemy position with their Lee Enfields (4) while the Bren gunner (5) keeps up a continuous stream of fire to pinpoint the suspected enemy position for the supporting Sherman (1) to engage with its 75mm main gun. Another rifleman (6) and a private armed with a PIAT hand-held anti-tank weapon (7) watch for the tell-tale muzzle flashes from other enemy positions. (Peter Dennis)

Infantry from British 3rd Division under fire during their advance near Caen. The regimental flash of a small, white rose of York on their sleeves denote that they are from 2nd East Yorks, 8th Brigade. The troops are wearing the new Mark III helmet that was issued to all troops who took part in the assault on D-Day. (IWM B7683)

the designated bombing area in the northern suburbs of Caen, a full six kilometres behind the enemy lines, hoping to prevent the enemy from bringing forward reinforcements during the night.

At 21.50hrs, as the bombers passed overhead, artillery opened up on the known sites of the enemy's anti-aircraft guns. The heavy bombing raid lasted an hour, then came the light bombers of No. 2 Group RAF who attacked areas further to the rear and enemy troop movements. At 23.00hrs the artillery of I and VIII Corps and the naval guns of the warships began to lay down a barrage on Caen and the fortified villages that surrounded the city. This firing went on throughout the night, and then, at 04.20hrs on 8 July all the artillery switched to the enemy positions right in the front line. A little later, British 3rd and 59th Divisions moved out of their trenches and attacked.

British 3rd Division stormed through the village of Lébisey which it had watched impotently for the past four weeks and pushed on down the road into Caen, while 59th Division rose from its line around Cambes and attacked La Bijude and Galmanche. At 07.00hrs the bombers were back. Fighter-bombers and rocket-firing Typhoons from RAF Second Tactical Air Force strafed the rear areas and 250 medium bombers from US Ninth Air Force bombed roads, bridges and German forming-up areas. It seemed that there was to be no end to Caen's suffering, nor for the 20,000 French civilians still sheltering in the city.

The Canadians in the west joined in the battle at 07.30hrs, attacking the villages of Buron and Gruchy, the site of their bloody rebuff a month earlier. All the artillery now switched to the area to support the move. Throughout the day, Canadian 3rd Division pressed 12th SS-Panzer Division but the 'Hitlerjugend' Panzergrenadiers were determined to hold out to the last. Each yard of ground had to be torn from their control by force. By 08.30hrs Buron was in Canadian hands and remained so despite numerous counterattacks during the morning. Thirteen enemy tanks were knocked out during the struggle for Buron, while the squadron of Shermans, supporting the Highland Light Infantry of Canada in the attack, lost 11 of its tanks. The Canadians swept on southwards, taking Authie and then Franqueville before joining up with the troops in

EVENTS

1. 05.00HRS, 10 JULY. After a barrage by over 100 guns, the lead battalions of Brig Mole's 129th Brigade move out across open cornfields into the attack, supported by the Churchill tanks of 31st Tank Brigade. The 5th Wiltshires reach the German defences just in front of the Éterville-Evrecy road but are forced to a halt by the enemy's defences.

2. In the centre of 129th Brigade's attack, 4th Somerset Light Infantry reach the main road but are unable to break through the German line to get onto the summit of Hill 112. As with all of the attacks, the Churchill tanks are unable to survive on the open hillside and numbers of them are knocked out, forcing the survivors to retreat to hull-down positions further back.

3. The third battalion of 129th Brigade, 4th Wiltshires, break through the German main line, but are held up just short of the road by enemy counterattacks.

4. Attacking abreast of 129th Brigade with the support of 4th Armoured Brigade, the 5th Dorsets of 130th Brigade advance and capture Chateau de Fontaine after much heavy fighting, but are unable to press on any further towards the main road.

5. With troops in Chateau de Fontaine, Brig Leslie, commander of 130th Brigade, launches an attack against Éterville with 4th Dorsets and the Churchill tanks of 4th Armoured Brigade. The battalion gets into the village but takes all morning to clear the enemy from the houses.

6. 08.15HRS. 7th Hampshires advance behind a rolling barrage between Éterville and Chateau de Fontaine and attack Maltot. The troops come under accurate enemy mortar fire as they move across the 2,000 metres of open cornfields and have great difficulty in taking the village. Before they can secure their position, they are counterattacked by SS Panzergrenadiers from 12th SS-Panzer Division and are driven into a small area near the crossroads. Their commanding officer, LtCol Ray is killed and contact is lost with brigade HQ.

7. 09.15HRS. 2nd Glasgow Highlanders and the 7th Seaforth Highlanders of 46th Brigade attack eastwards astride the River Odon. Later in the day they link up with 3rd Canadian Division in Bretteville sur Odon to secure the eastern flank of the operation.

8. SS Panzergrenadiers and Tiger tanks from 102nd SS Heavy Tank Battalion counterattack 7th Hampshires again. Unable to hold the village, the survivors begin to withdraw during the afternoon.

9. 9th Cameronians, 46th Brigade, relieve 4th Dorsets in Éterville. Unaware of the Hampshires' withdrawal, 4th Dorsets move across to Maltot to support the beleaguered battalion. They are met by furious enemy fire and counterattacks during the afternoon and are virtually wiped out. Those men that survive stagger back to Éterville.

10. The loss of Maltot forces MajGen Thomas to bring forward two battalions from his reserve brigade, Brig Essame's 214th Brigade, to hold the reverse slope against an armoured counterattack by the enemy. The 7th Somerset Light Infantry are brought into the line to the east of Chateau de Fontaine, and 1st Worcestershires to the west of this position alongside the hard pressed 4th Wiltshires, to secure the gains made earlier in the day. Both battalions are shelled and mortared incessantly, the 7th Somersets losing their commander, LtCol Lance, killed.

11. Enemy counterattacks and shelling stall 43rd Division's advance all along the line. At 15.00hrs, MajGen Thomas realises that only a fresh attack on Hill 112 can stabilise the situation. He orders his one remaining battalion, 5th Duke of Cornwall's Light Infantry to attack and occupy the summit. At 20.30hrs the attack goes in behind a rolling artillery barrage. The Cornishmen advance with the support of tanks from 31st Tank Brigade through withering enemy fire and manage get into the wood on the top of the hill.

12. Tanks and Panzergrenadiers from 10th SS-Panzer Division counterattack the Cornwalls during the night. The attack is beaten off with heavy loss.

13. Further attacks on the summit are put in throughout the night, including one by the Tiger tanks of 102nd SS-Heavy Tank Battalion. Enemy troops manage to establish themselves in the southern side of the small wood and small arms fire and mortars pound the Duke of Cornwall's Light Infantry into the early hours.

14. Just before dawn on 11 July, Panzergrenadiers from 9th SS-Panzer Division move onto the western slopes of Hill 112 ready to attack, but are themselves attacked at first light by a squadron of tanks from the Royal Scots Greys of 4th Armoured Brigade, who have come forward to join the Cornwalls. The Scots Greys clear the enemy from the wood, but lose so many tanks in the process that the squadron is withdrawn back down the hill.

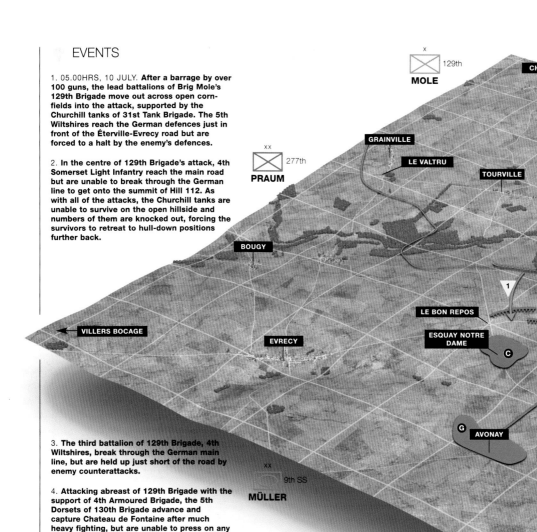

58

OPERATION JUPITER – THE ATTACK ON HILL 112

10–11 July 1944, viewed from the south-east, showing the desperate struggle as British 43rd (Wessex) Division attempts to seize Hill 112, Éterville and Maltot and push on to the River Orne. It is halted by counterattacks by three different Waffen-SS divisions.

Note: Gridlines are shown at intervals of 1km/0.62 miles

BRITISH FORCES

129th Brigade
1   5th Wiltshires
2   4th Somerset Light Infantry
3   4th Wiltshires

130th Brigade
4   5th Dorsets
5   7th Hampshires
6   4th Dorsets

46th Brigade
7   Seaforth Highlanders
8   Glasgow Highlanders

214th Brigade
9   5th Duke of Cornwall's Light Infantry
10 1st Worcesters
11 7th Somerset Light Infantry

GERMAN FORCES

10th SS-Panzer Division 'Frundsberg'
A   I Battalion, 22nd SS-Panzergrenadier Regiment
B   II Battalion, 21st SS-Panzergrenadier Regiment
C   21st SS-Panzergrenadier Regiment (elements)
D   5th Company, 10th SS-Panzer Regiment

12th SS-Panzer Divison 'Hitlerjugend'
E   5th Company, 12th SS-Panzer Regiment
F   102nd SS-Heavy Tank Battalion

9th SS-Panzer Division 'Hohenstaufen'
G   19th SS-Panzergrenadier Regiment

Map labels: 4th CARVER, 130th LESLIE, 43rd THOMAS, 46th BARBER, 214th ESSAME, VERSON, FONTAINE ÉTOUPFOUR, CHÂTEAU DE FONTAINE, ÉTERVILLE, CAEN, MALTOT, ST MARTIN, FEUGUEROLLES, ST ANDRÉ, MAY, ST ANDRÉ, 12th SS WITT, I SS DIETRICH, 10th SS HARMEL

15. With the coming of daylight the enemy artillery fire increases. The Cornwall's commanding officer, LtCol James, is killed whilst directing artillery fire and the end is now in sight for the isolated men of the Wessex Division. Their position is untenable. During the morning, those who have survived, just 80 men out of the 400 who set out the day before, are called back down off the summit and into reserve.

16. The summit of Hill 112 remained a no-man's-land, with neither side able to withstand the artillery fire of both armies that pounds the hill. Operation Jupiter stutters to a halt with heavy losses. The 43rd Wessex Division now digs in and establishes a secure line on the reverse slope to deny the enemy possession of the barren wasteland of Hill 112.

Royal Canadian Engineers clearing rubble from the streets of Caen. It was important to get roads opened quickly so that troops and tanks could get forward to the bridges over the Orne in the city. (Ken Bell, NAC 169342)

Carpiquet. Then they turned eastwards, heading for the infamous Ardenne Abbey, the headquarters of 25th SS-Panzergrenadier Regiment since D-Day and the site of the massacre of Canadian prisoners by 'Panzer' Meyer's teenage fanatics. As darkness fell, the Regina Rifles advanced across open fields through withering fire to close on the abbey. Pounded, bombed and gradually surrounded, the SS troops withdrew back into Caen, taking with them the exposed garrison from the hangars on the eastern side of Carpiquet airfield.

To the Canadians' left, 59th Division was compelled to fight hard for the fortifications and trench systems of the string of villages that barred its way. La Bijude, Epron, Galmanche and St Contest were all attacked with great force, but the SS troops defending the villages fought with

British troops in the ruins of Caen keep watch for enemy armour armed with a hand-held PIAT anti-tank weapon. This weapon was unable to penetrate most German tanks unless the PIAT gunner could manoeuvre for a side or rear shot at close range. (IWM B6899)

fanatical determination. By the end of the day the division had not advanced more than a mile from its start line. Further to the east, British 3rd Division had fought doggedly against the gradually weakening Luftwaffe troops and was pressing into the outskirts of the city, amid the devastation caused by the heavy bombers. The debris blocking every street slowed progress to a crawl.

During the night and into the next day, the bombers of Second Tactical Air Force returned, churning up more debris, pouncing on any enemy concentrations and, tragically, killing more Frenchmen. Caen was about to fall. The weight of fire and the pressure of three divisions grinding inexorably forward brought this realisation home to the commander of Army Group B. Rommel ordered that all heavy weapons from the three corps in the area, LXXXVI, I and II SS-Panzer Corps, should be withdrawn from the city during the night. Infantry and engineer groups were to remain until attacked by superior Allied forces when they were to withdraw through the city to a new line along the southern bank of the River Orne.

Early on 9 July the ground attack resumed. Bomb craters, fallen rubble and collapsed buildings made progress slow, and snipers and mortars caused problems, but the three divisions of I Corps pushed steadily on towards the city centre. The Canadians also swept down the western side of Caen and reached the Odon, taking control of Carpiquet airfield and the village of Bretteville sur Odon. Mopping up in Caen continued throughout the day as the enemy gradually withdrew in front of the rapidly increasing numbers of infantry pouring into the city, then, at last, Caen was deemed to be in British hands. At least, the area of the city north of the Orne was in British hands; the enemy still stubbornly defended the factory areas and suburbs on the other side of the river.

The butcher's bill for the capture of Caen was high. British I Corps had taken almost 3,500 casualties. Eighty Allied tanks had been destroyed or were out of action. German 16th Luftwaffe Division had lost 75 per cent of its strength. The once-powerful 12th SS-Panzer Division 'Hitlerjugend', could only muster the combined strength of a single infantry battalion. For the French, three-quarters of their city was in ruins, over 1,000 of them were dead and tens of thousands had been made homeless. Liberation had come at a high price.

Operation Jupiter: The Attack on Hill 112

While British Second Army had been slogging away at Caen, the Americans on the other side of the lodgement had encountered their own problems in securing ground in which to manoeuvre. The town of St Lô was proving every bit as difficult for the Americans to capture as Caen was for the British. However, the military situation in the American sector was improving for the Allies. Bradley's First Army had battered the town to the edge of oblivion and was on the point of capturing its shattered ruins. This would allow Bradley to push south to gain room in which to deploy the newly arriving US Third Army and prepare it for the great 'break-out' battle that would release Allied forces into the heartland of France. Whilst these preliminary moves were in progress, it was important that Montgomery kept the bulk of the German armour engaged with his Second Army. This would help reduce the opposition faced by Bradley's American forces. It was vital LtGen Dempsey

5TH WILTSHIRES' ATTACK ON HILL 112, 10 JULY 1944
(pages 62–63)

The strategically important Hill 112, which dominated the ground to the west of Caen and gave clear observation over British lines all the way to the coast, had been occupied and then given up during Operation Epsom in late June. On 10 July, British 43rd Wessex Division was ordered to regain the hill in order to open a way down to the River Orne to enable troops to push across to the south of Caen. The scene shows the extreme right-hand sector of the divisional attack, with men from 5th Wiltshires of 129th Brigade advancing out of their positions near Baron supported by Churchill tanks of 7th Royal Tank Regiment. The relatively heavily armoured and ponderous Churchill tank (1) was an infantry tank designed to give close support to these ground troops, able to get close to the enemy and engage targets of opportunity. The plan of attack was for artillery and mortar fire to saturate enemy defences while infantry and tanks advanced across the open cornfields to close on their positions. The armour and infantry would then the German defences allowing follow-up troops to pass through and exploit. The battle for Hill 112 was an example of brute force and numbers trying to overcome an entrenched enemy. In the event,neither the bombardment nor the attack dislodged the enemy troops who stayed resolutely at their post returning fire. On the left of 129th Brigade, 130th Brigade attacked the villages of Eterville (2) and Maltot (3) to the east of Hill 112, but although Eterville was taken and held, 7th Hampshires were unable to seize and hold the burning village of Maltot. The 5th Wiltshires in their attack advanced no further than the road that runs across the

upper part of the hill (4) where they were forced to dig in and endure heavy shelling by the enemy. The 4th Somerset Light Infantry (5), advancing to the left of 5th Wiltshires, were likewise unable to reach the summit of Hill 112. In the evening, during a renewed attack, the 5th Duke of Cornwall's Light Infantry passed through the Somersets and reached the copse at the top of the hill (6), only to be ejected by the enemy the following day. The entire summit was then subjected to almost constant shelling by both sides. For Corporal Vic Coombs (7) and the men of A Company of 5th Wiltshires, this was their first major attack. They had taken part in Operation Epsom, but mostly in a defensive role. The attack on Hill 112 was costly for the battalion, which lost 120 men killed, wounded and missing, but the casualties were only half those lost by most of the other battalions in the division during this attack. The 5th Duke of Cornwall's Light Infantry suffered 320 casualties, including 90 men killed. By the end of the three days of Operation Jupiter, the battle to take Hill 112, the Wessex Division had over 2,000 casualties. For Vic Coombs, his war continued through the Normandy fighting taking part in various attacks including the famous capture of Mont Pinçon where his colonel was killed alongside him as he urged his men over a small bridge at the base of the hill. At Vernon on the River Seine in August 1944, Corporal Vic Coombs was with A Company as it led the assault waves of the battalion across the river in storm boats. During the crossing and on the far shore virtually the entire company was wiped out, with every man killed, wounded or captured. Vic Coombs was one of the very few lucky men who escaped death, but spent the remainder of the war in captivity. (Peter Dennis)

The River Orne, which runs through the centre of Caen. By the time that I Corps troops arrived on the river the enemy had blown the three bridges that link the city to the industrial areas of Mondeville, Colombelles and Vaucelles. (Ken Bell, NAC PA 114508)

maintained the pressure on the enemy Panzer divisions and continued to threaten a breakthrough around Caen.

The capture of northern Caen now allowed Montgomery to consider enlarging the British flank of the landings with a double envelopment around the south of Caen intending to break through the German cordon and get onto the plain in front of Falaise. In any event, such an attack would prevent the enemy from disengaging any of his armoured formations to transfer them to the American sector. Before this ambitious operation could be put into effect, the enemy had to be pinned in place on the Orne. Montgomery told Dempsey to send VIII Corps onto the offensive again and try to advance out of the salient seized during Operation Epsom and get down to the River Orne.

The small bridgehead south of the Odon captured by 15th Scottish and 11th Armoured Divisions was to be expanded to capture Eterville, Maltot and to recapture Hill 112, given up at the end of Epsom. Infantry and armour were then to descend into the Orne valley and seize crossings over the river. This task was given to 43rd Wessex Division, which had played a consolidating role during VIII Corps' earlier operation and was still relatively fresh. The Wessex Division would be backed up by the tanks of 4th Armoured and 31st Tank Brigades. The usual lavish artillery support would be on hand from the guns of 43rd, 15th and 11th Armoured Divisions, together with the heavier weight of the medium and heavy weapons of 3rd and 8th Army Groups Royal Artillery (AGRAs).

Hill 112 dominates all the ground for kilometres around with clear views as far as the sea in the north and towards Caen. Its strategic importance was not lost on the enemy. Rommel had once said that he who holds Hill 112 holds Normandy. When 11th Armoured Division managed to get tanks onto its southern slopes in late June, it had triggered alarm bells within the German command. At the end of Operation Epsom, when the British pulled off the hill back into their bridgehead over the Odon at Buron, the site was immediately reoccupied by the enemy and fortified with minefields, trenches and dug-in gun positions.

Operation Jupiter began the day after Caen had fallen, 10 July, when an artillery barrage beat a path in front of the two lead brigades of 43rd Division as they began their attack. With 129th Brigade on the right and 130th Brigade on the left, six battalions of the Wessex Division advanced up the long slopes of Hill 112 into terrible small arms and artillery fire laid down by 10th SS-Panzer Division. SS snipers and machine-gunners were hidden in the high corn and did fearful damage to the Allied troops that passed by at close quarters. 130th Brigade took the first villages of Eterville and Fontaine Etoupefour, and the 7th Hampshires pushed on to Maltot overlooking the Orne, but enemy counterattacks by 12th SS-Panzer Division evicted them in the early afternoon after virtually wiping out the entire battalion. At the same time 4th Dorsets advanced into the eastern end of the village in an attempt to help rescue the Hampshires, but when the Dorsets entered the village it was full of SS troops; the Hampshires had already been destroyed.

On the right, 129th Brigade reached the road crossing Hill 112 beneath its crest but was unable to get across and onto the summit. Tank support could not survive in the open and tens of Churchills and Shermans were left blazing in the golden corn. Major-General Thomas ordered 214th Brigade up onto the hill and sent 5th Duke of Cornwall's Light Infantry (DCLI) to seize the small copse on the top in the early evening. Here the Cornishmen were repeatedly attacked by troops of both 9th and 10th SS-Panzer divisions and Tiger tanks from schwere SS-Panzer Abteilung 101. The 5th Cornwalls held on throughout the night and tanks from the Scots Greys reached the small wood in the morning mist to support them, but the loss of 5th DCLI's commanding officer and further enemy attacks made continued possession of the summit impossible. The few men of the battalion that had survived the night were pulled off the hill and it was once again given up.

Neither side, however, allowed the other possession of Hill 112. The entire hill including the small wood that sat squarely on its summit was subjected to continual bombardment by the British and the Germans

OPERATION GOODWOOD – PLAN OF ATTACK

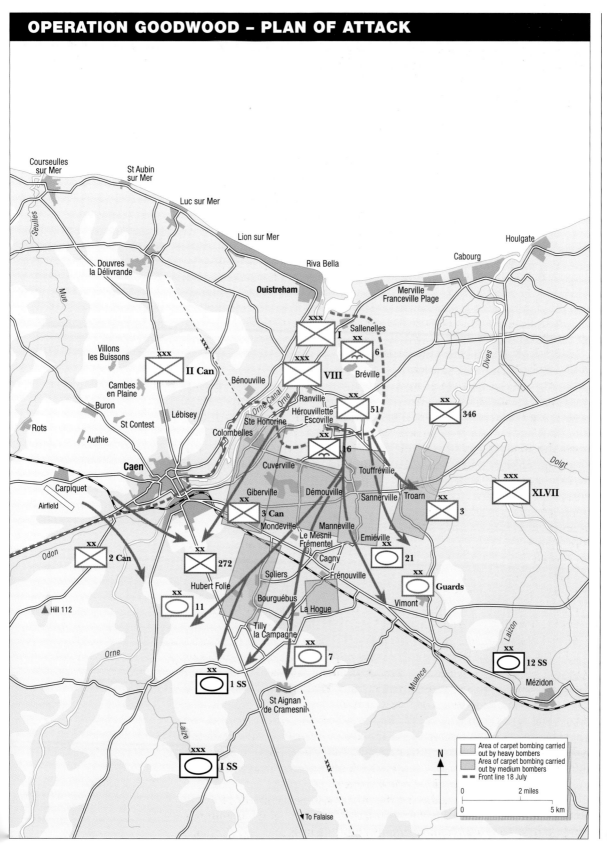

Courseulles sur Mer
St Aubin sur Mer
Luc sur Mer
Lion sur Mer
Riva Bella
Houlgate
Cabourg
Douvres la Délivrande
Ouistreham
Merville Franceville Plage
Villons les Buissons
XXX
II Can
Bénouville
XXX
I
Sallenelles
XX
6
XXX
VIII
Bréville
XX
51
XX
346
Cambes en Plaine
Buron
St Contest
Lébisey
Ranville
Hérouvillette
Escoville
Ste Honorine
Rots
Authie
Colombelles
XX
16
Touffréville
Doigt
Caen
Cuvérville
Sannerville
Troarn
XXX
XLVII
Carpiquet Airfield
Giberville
Démouville
XX
3
XX
3 Can
Mondeville
Manneville
Le Mesnil Frémentel
Emiéville
XX
21
XX
2 Can
XX
272
Cagny
Frénouville
XX
Guards
Hubert Folie
Soliers
Vimont
Hill 112
XX
11
Bourguébus
La Hogue
Tilly la Campagne
XX
7
XX
12 SS
Mézidon
Orne
XX
1 SS
St Aignan de Cramesnil
XXX
I SS
To Falaise

N

Area of carpet bombing carried out by heavy bombers
Area of carpet bombing carried out by medium bombers
Front line 18 July

0   2 miles
0   5 km

67

alike. The hill was reduced to a barren, shell-torn no-man's-land upon which no living thing could survive. Operation Jupiter was called to a halt on 12 July after just two days. It had been another costly failure, gaining a few more rubble-strewn villages in which the occupying troops were forced to live a miserable existence under constant shellfire, but pushing only a little nearer to the Orne. The cost to the Wessex Division was fearful: over 2,000 casualties in this its first battle.

OPERATION GOODWOOD

Operation Goodwood was to be Montgomery's greatest offensive in Normandy. Three of his five corps would attack the enemy from the bridgehead gained on the eastern side of the Orne Canal. The main blow would be made by VIII Corps, which now contained the three British armoured divisions in Normandy: the Guards, and 7th and 11th Armoured Divisions. These would drive south-west from the line held by 51st Highland Division, through the main German defence positions and make for the Caen–Falaise road to establish themselves on the high ground to the south of the city. The charge of these armoured divisions would hit the enemy with speed and strength, spreading disorder within his broken line. Armoured cars would then be free to harass the enemy in his rear towards Falaise.

I Corps and Canadian II Corps would protect VIII Corps' flanks. When VIII Corps attacked, Crocker's 3rd Division would advance on the left seizing the villages that overlooked the route of the armoured columns. On the right, Canadian 3rd Division from Canadian II Corps would attack alongside VIII Corps, taking the village of Giberville, the giant steel works at Colombelles and the industrial area of Mondeville. At the same time Canadian 2nd Division would force crossings over the River Orne in Caen itself and to the west of the city to meet up with its sister division's advance from the north.

General Montgomery discusses the forthcoming offensive with LtGen Crocker, Commander British I Corps. (IWM 6931)

A private soldier poses for the camera in a street in Caen after the city had been captured by I Corps. (IWM B6725)

Operation Goodwood would be a mailed fist striking hard at a defence line held by three German infantry divisions. At the western end of this line was 272nd Division facing the Canadians in Caen. To the east and north, facing British 51st division, was the depleted 16th Luftwaffe Field Division, still reeling from the hammering it had received in Caen during Operation Charnwood. Lastly and furthest east, overlooking 6th Airborne Division, was German 346th Division. South of the German lines were the Panzer divisions that could move forward as required: 21st Panzer Division in the east and 1st SS-Panzer Division in the south-west. 12th SS-Panzer Division was gradually withdrawing to Lisieux for a rest. The Germans had at last been able to pull their Panzers out of the frontline and now had a classic defence with infantry divisions holding the line and mobile armoured forces ready to react to any Allied breakthrough

Also distributed throughout this sector were elements of Gen Pickert's Luftwaffe III Flak Corps with their dual-purpose 88mm guns. The multi-barrelled mortars of 7th and 9th Werfer Brigades added to the firepower. These formations put a total of 194 extra pieces of artillery and 272 Nebelwerfer mortars in the sector, in addition to the weapons of the existing divisions. Also defending the centre of the sector was schwere Panzer Abteilung 503, which had recently equipped one of its companies with the massive new Panzerkampfwagen VI Tiger Ausf.B, known as the 'Kingtiger'. Panzer Group West had in total around 230 tanks facing Second Army on the east of the Orne – Panzer IVs, Panthers and Tiger Is and IIs – almost all of which were superior to the standard Cromwells and Shermans of the British. To counter this qualitative imbalance, VIII Corps would put 750 tanks into its attack, while a further 350 tanks supported the flanking movements on either side.

Even after six weeks of heavy fighting the Germans were still able to field a powerful force with which to counter the expected British attack. On paper at least, the totals looked formidable, but the Allies still held the all-important superiority in the air. The sky above Normandy belonged to the RAF and USAAF. Operation Goodwood was to be preceded by another great display of aerial might. A programme of bombing raids, bigger, longer and heavier than any that had gone before, was to be laid on prior to the attack. Over 1,000 bombers were to drop thousands of

Monument to 43rd Wessex Division on the site of its costliest battle. The granite memorial lies just below the summit of Hill 112 with the small copse captured and then lost by 5th Duke of Cornwall's Light Infantry visible in the background. The division lost over 2,000 men in just two days of fighting. (Ken Ford)

Tanks move forward over the River Orne into the airborne bridgehead east of Caen in preparation for Operation Goodwood. (IWM B7503)

tons of bombs on villages, road centres and great tracts of land that might be sheltering German troops, to pulverise the enemy into a state of stunned shock before the tanks rolled across the start line. With the forces in front of them destroyed or disorganised, the armoured columns would then rush on to their objectives, pushing aside any surviving pockets of resistance for the infantry to mop up later. At least that was the plan.

The Goodwood offensive would finally give Montgomery Caen. The attack would take the whole of the city, the industrial areas to the east and the ground to the south. At last, Caen would be encircled with Allied troops. The moves were sure to provoke the enemy into very spirited resistance, counterattacking the advance wherever he could. The German Panzer divisions known to be in the area would inevitably be drawn into the battle. Also shifting eastwards against the moves, if

The Orne Canal at Bénouville beside Pegasus Bridge, the location of the two Bailey bridges that were put over the water obstacle to help carry the three armoured divisions forward to their forming-up places for Operation Goodwood. The small size of the bridgehead to the east of the Orne and the need to keep knowledge of the build-up from the enemy, meant that the three armoured divisions of VIII Corps and the infantry of Canadian 3rd Division all had to cross the bridges one after the other and be fed straight into the battle. Not surprisingly, this led to some dreadful traffic congestion (Ken Ford)

they were permitted to do so, would be the tanks of II SS-Panzer Corps facing British XII Corps in the Odon sector. Montgomery knew that he had to keep the enemy to the west of Caen engaged to prevent them joining in the Goodwood battle, or worse still, moving westwards against the Americans who were still preparing for their break-out. To prevent this happening he ordered Dempsey to attack with XII and XXX Corps just prior to the start date of the Goodwood offensive, 18 July, in order to keep the enemy busy in the Odon and Caumont–Rauray areas.

On 15 July, Dempsey's two British corps attacked in the western part of the British sector as Montgomery had instructed. They fought against a determined and well-entrenched enemy fighting over ground previously contested during the past three weeks. XII Corps pushed along the southern side of the Odon valley and took Bougy and Gavrus with 15th Scottish Division, while 53rd Welsh Division attacked up the other side of the river. Both divisions were counterattacked and halted. On their right, 49th and 59th Divisions attempted to extend XXX Corps' line by taking Vendes, Haut des Forges and Noyers-Bocage. There were mixed results, 59th Division took Haut des Forges, but could not seize and hold Noyers, and 49th Division took Vendes after two days of fighting. On the extreme right, 50th Division managed to capture Hottot a village that had defied it for more than a month.

These attacks committed five divisions, gained little new territory and cost over 3,500 casualties. On the plus side they had achieved most of what Montgomery had asked of them. The 10th SS-Panzer and 2nd Panzer Divisions had been kept west of Caen and the threats posed in this sector by the British attacks had drawn 9th SS-Panzer Division out of II Corps' reserves and even brought across elements of 1st SS-Panzer Division from the east to counter them. The two German infantry divisions in the line, 276th and 277th, had also been badly mauled. It was now time for Montgomery to move his armoured divisions over the Orne Canal and push them into the battle to break the German line on the eastern side of Caen.

The day before Goodwood opened, 17 July, two Typhoon fighter-bombers from the RAF inflicted a significant loss on the enemy, but at the time the pilots concerned were not aware of it. Just outside the town of Livarot, 14km to the east of St Pierre sur Dives, at around 18.00hrs the aircraft spotted a German staff car moving at speed towards the town. They swooped down and strafed the vehicle sending it crashing into a ditch throwing its passengers out and killing the driver. One of the injured was Generalfeldmarschall Rommel. He was unconscious for a week and spent several more weeks recovering from his injuries. Immediately after the accident, Von Kluge took over duties as Commander Amy Group B as well as remaining C-in-C (West). Rommel never returned to the battlefield; on 20 July an assassination attempt was made on the Führer in what became known as 'the July bomb plot'. Hitler survived, apparently miraculously, and what followed was a witch-hunt throughout the German army. Rommel was implicated in the plot and forced to commit suicide on 14 October, ending the life and career of one of Germany's most successful battlefield commanders.

The opening moves of Operation Goodwood began on the night of 17 July as the component parts of VIII Corps moved across the lodgement from west to east and gathered ready to cross the River Orne and its canal. The airborne bridgehead on the other side was too cramped to allow three armoured divisions to assemble for the attack. Their concentration south of Ranville would also give warning to the enemy of the direction and axis of a forthcoming operation. It was

The village of Sannerville on the east of the battle area after it had been attacked by the heavy bombers of the RAF on 18 July at the start of Operation Goodwood. The village was blanketed with thousands of tons of high explosive and fragmentation bombs, shattering the German defences and field fortifications and leaving a dense concentration of deep craters. (IWM CL 476)

The effects of the heavy bombing raid on Sannerville. The railway line through the village has been torn apart and the whole area was covered with overlapping craters. (IWM B7576)

therefore decided that they would be brought round to the north of Caen and would then cross over the two waterways at the appropriate time and in the order they were to be introduced into the battle. Another factor affecting the timings of the moves was that there were only three available routes across the river and canal: the original canal and river bridges at Bénouville, seized in a *coup de main* by the airborne on 6 June, and the four Bailey bridges erected by Royal Engineers after D-Day. The introduction of the three armoured divisions into the largest attack so far in Normandy, would now appear to be dependent on the Allies' ability to avoid traffic jams.

The Great Bomber Raids

At 05.30hrs on a beautiful summer's morning, the artillery of three entire Corps opened fire on known German anti-aircraft defences. Shortly afterwards ears could detect a distant hum, which quickly became an insistent roar as hundreds of Lancaster and Halifax bombers from the Royal Air Force swept into view from the north. Inexorably, through long, snaking lines of tracer and black puffs of enemy flak, the aircraft pressed on to their targets. The steelworks at Colombelles and the line of villages from Touffréville to Emiéville in the east, disappeared under a deluge of high explosives. On each of these target areas, the RAF dropped 2,500 tons of bombs. Further to the south, the fortified village of Cagny was the target of 500 tons of explosives. Those German Flak gunners that had escaped the opening barrage accounted for six aircraft shot down.

When the heavy bombers had turned for home, it was the turn of the mediums. At 07.00hrs the B-26 Marauders of US Ninth Air Force flew in trying to find their targets in the clouds of dust and smoke that hung over the battlefield. They attacked a designated 'box' of ground outlined by the four villages of Cuverville, Sannerville, Manneville and Démouville, which were right in the path of the planned advance of the armoured divisions.

Troops and tanks move forward at the start of Operation Goodwood on 18 July. No markings are visible to indicate the Sherman's unit, but the tank appears to have been named 'Accuser'. (IWM B7577)

EVENTS

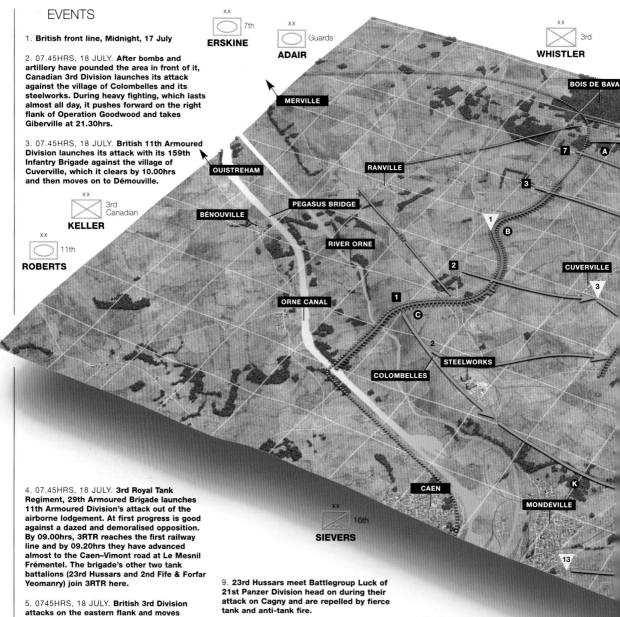

ERSKINE — 7th XX

ADAIR — Guards XX

WHISTLER — 3rd XX

BOIS DE BAVA

MERVILLE

RANVILLE

OUISTREHAM

PEGASUS BRIDGE

BÉNOUVILLE

RIVER ORNE

KELLER — 3rd Canadian XX

ROBERTS — 11th XX

CUVERVILLE

ORNE CANAL

STEELWORKS

COLOMBELLES

CAEN

MONDEVILLE

SIEVERS — 16th XX

1. **British front line, Midnight, 17 July**

2. 07.45HRS, 18 JULY. **After bombs and artillery have pounded the area in front of it, Canadian 3rd Division launches its attack against the village of Colombelles and its steelworks. During heavy fighting, which lasts almost all day, it pushes forward on the right flank of Operation Goodwood and takes Giberville at 21.30hrs.**

3. 07.45HRS, 18 JULY. **British 11th Armoured Division launches its attack with its 159th Infantry Brigade against the village of Cuverville, which it clears by 10.00hrs and then moves on to Démouville.**

4. 07.45HRS, 18 JULY. **3rd Royal Tank Regiment, 29th Armoured Brigade launches 11th Armoured Division's attack out of the airborne lodgement. At first progress is good against a dazed and demoralised opposition. By 09.00hrs, 3RTR reaches the first railway line and by 09.20hrs they have advanced almost to the Caen–Vimont road at Le Mesnil Frémentel. The brigade's other two tank battalions (23rd Hussars and 2nd Fife & Forfar Yeomanry) join 3RTR here.**

5. 0745HRS, 18 JULY. **British 3rd Division attacks on the eastern flank and moves against the villages Touffréville and Sannerville, making good progress against shattered opposition.**

6. 09.30HRS. **3 RTR and 2nd Fife & Forfar Yeomanry move across the Caen–Vimont railway line and fan out towards Grentheville and Soliers, while 23rd Hussars turns against Cagny.**

7. **On the open ground to the south of the railway line, the tanks of 3RTR and 2nd Fife & Forfar Yeomanry are hit by accurate tank and anti-tank fire from the surrounding villages and from 88mm guns on the Bourguébus ridge. 3RTR is forced to break of its attack on Hubert Folie.**

8. **2nd Fife & Forfar Yeomanry attack through Four and are caught by enemy artillery and tank fire as they head for Bourguébus, forcing them back to the railway line with heavy losses.**

9. **23rd Hussars meet Battlegroup Luck of 21st Panzer Division head on during their attack on Cagny and are repelled by fierce tank and anti-tank fire.**

10. **Late morning, 18 July. Fighter-bombers and British tank and anti-tank fire repel counterattacks by 1 SS-Panzer Division.**

11. **5th Armoured Brigade of the Guards Armoured Division attack Cagny and try to breakthrough along the road to Vimont but are held by 21st Panzer Division.**

12. **185th Brigade, British 3rd Division advances to the outskirts of Emiéville by early evening and secures the eastern flank of the attack.**

13. 18 JULY. **Canadian 2nd Division attacks across the River Orne from the centre of Caen.**

14. 19 JULY. **32nd Guards Brigade, the infantry brigade of the Guards Division, attempts to take Frénouville and Le Poirier, but the arrival of 12th-SS Panzer Division has strengthened the German defences.**

15. 16.00HRS, 19 JULY. **11th Armoured Division resumes its attack with a move against Bras. The village is captured at the second attempt and the division advances to take Hubert-Folie from 1st SS-Panzer Division that evening.**

16. **Canadian 3rd Division continue to attack southwards to take Mondeville and clear the industrial areas of Caen east of the Orne.**

17. AFTERNOON, 19 JULY. **Canadian 2nd Division's leading brigade is in Cormelles.**

18. MIDDAY, 19 JULY. **7th Armoured Division take Soliers and attempts to advance on Bourguébus but is repulsed by 1st SS-Panzer Division.**

19. 16.00HRS, 19 JULY. **An attack on La Hogue by 7th Armoured Division is repulsed, but an immediate German counterattack from this area by 1st SS-Panzer Division is beaten off.**

OPERATION GOODWOOD

18–21 July 1944, viewed from the south-west, showing Montgomery's biggest offensive in the battle for Caen. Supported by elements of I Corps and Canadian II Corps, VIII Corps attack out of the airborne bridgehead east of the Orne in an attempt to break through to the Caen–Falaise road.

Note: Gridlines are shown at intervals of 1km/0.62 miles

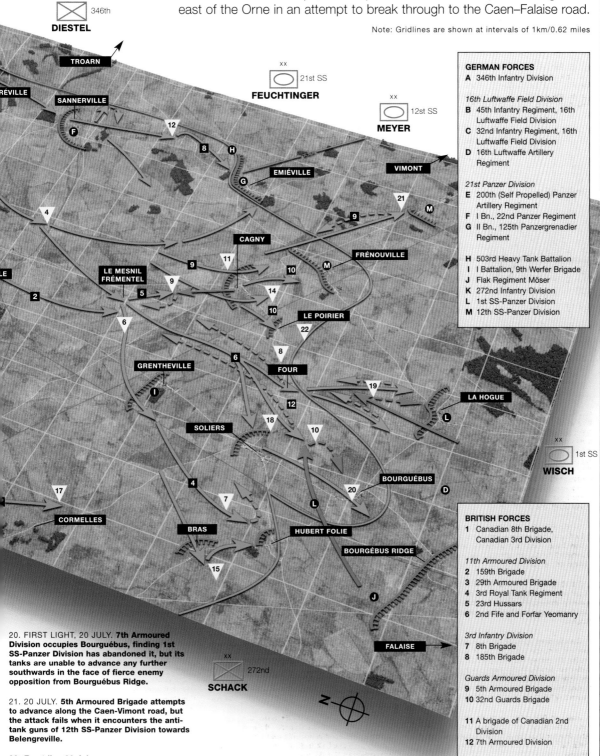

GERMAN FORCES
A 346th Infantry Division

16th Luftwaffe Field Division
B 45th Infantry Regiment, 16th Luftwaffe Field Division
C 32nd Infantry Regiment, 16th Luftwaffe Field Division
D 16th Luftwaffe Artillery Regiment

21st Panzer Division
E 200th (Self Propelled) Panzer Artillery Regiment
F I Bn., 22nd Panzer Regiment
G II Bn., 125th Panzergrenadier Regiment

H 503rd Heavy Tank Battalion
I I Battalion, 9th Werfer Brigade
J Flak Regiment Möser
K 272nd Infantry Division
L 1st SS-Panzer Division
M 12th SS-Panzer Division

BRITISH FORCES
1 Canadian 8th Brigade, Canadian 3rd Division

11th Armoured Division
2 159th Brigade
3 29th Armoured Brigade
4 3rd Royal Tank Regiment
5 23rd Hussars
6 2nd Fife and Forfar Yeomanry

3rd Infantry Division
7 8th Brigade
8 185th Brigade

Guards Armoured Division
9 5th Armoured Brigade
10 32nd Guards Brigade

11 A brigade of Canadian 2nd Division
12 7th Armoured Division

20. FIRST LIGHT, 20 JULY. **7th Armoured Division occupies Bourguébus, finding 1st SS-Panzer Division has abandoned it, but its tanks are unable to advance any further southwards in the face of fierce enemy opposition from Bourguébus Ridge.**

21. 20 JULY. **5th Armoured Brigade attempts to advance along the Caen-Vimont road, but the attack fails when it encounters the anti-tank guns of 12th SS-Panzer Division towards Belengreville.**

22. **Front line 20 July**

At 07.35hrs, the artillery resumed its bombardment. Once again the guns of the three Corps opened fire, this time concentrating on the positions of known enemy batteries. Their fire was augmented by the heavier weapons of the cruisers *Mauritius* and *Enterprise* and the monitor *Roberts*. At the same time the leading divisions moved out through pre-arranged gaps in the minefields and began the attack. Further to the south, the four-engined Liberator bombers of US Eighth Air Force lumbered over and dropped thousands more tons of bombs on a great swath of countryside from Grentheville to Bourguébus, the area to the south of the Caen–Vimont railway over which 11th Armoured Division must pass. Then it was time for the fighter-bombers of 83rd and 84th Groups RAF to swoop in and harass the enemy, a task they continued with for the remainder of the day.

While the tanks of 11th Armoured Division rolled out into the open country near Cuverville to open the main attack, the corps on either side of it had begun their advance along the flanks. On the Allied right Canadian 3rd Division supported by Canadian 2nd Armoured Brigade attacked towards the factory area of Colombelles. They advanced over ground that had been torn up by the

The village of Cagny on the morning of 18 July immediately after the raid by the heavy Halifax and Lancaster bombers of RAF Bomber Command. The area has been hit by bombs that have been fused to explode immediately they hit the ground in order not to form deep craters that might hold up Allied tanks. The blast rings from each impact can be clearly seen. (IWM CL477)

bombers leaving almost overlapping craters. At first progress was good through areas surrendered by the dazed survivors of 16th Luftwaffe Field Division and troops were soon in Giberville and the steelworks. Then resistance stiffened markedly, as Panzergrenadiers from 21st Panzer Division and infantry from 272nd Division came forward to strengthen the enemy's hold on Colombelles. Fighting continued all day and into the night, but the Canadians made steady progress southwards looking to link up with Canadian II Corps' other division attacking out of Caen across the Orne.

To the east, on 11th Armoured Division's left flank, British 3rd Division attacked out of the airborne bridgehead and moved against Touffréville. As with the other attacks that day, the infantry moved behind a steady rolling artillery barrage that blasted the already shaken enemy in front of it. The division attacked a line of villages leading southwards trying to keep pace with the movement by the armoured division in the centre. The villages that had been heavily bombed such as Sannerville and Banneville were taken relatively easily from the dazed German defenders, but those that had missed the weight of Bomber Command's raids, stubbornly refused to give up. Touffréville and Troarn proved to be difficult nuts to crack. Touffréville held out until nightfall, but Troarn remained untaken. By the end of the day, 3rd Division had troops on the outskirts of Emiéville in the south.

The Drive of the Armoured Divisions

The ground that 11th Armoured Division was attacking was open, flat farmland not cluttered by the thick hedges and sunken lanes that choked the battlefield on the other side of Caen. Visibility was good for kilometres, with just isolated villages scattered across the area. Cutting across the line of advance were two railway lines. The first, from Caen to

Cromwell tanks move forward in the early morning of 18 July from the airborne lodgement. In the far background can be seen the gliders used in the 6 June operation, left abandoned on the landing ground since D-Day. (IWM B7535)

Troarn, was two kilometres from the start line. The next, the railway from Caen to Vimont, was three kilometres beyond that.

With the supporting Corps taking care of the flanks, the role of Monty's armour was clear. 11th Armoured Division would lead the attack and drive southwards towards the area of Cagny, swing to the south-west to capture the villages of Soliers and Hubert Folie, then cross the Caen–Falaise highway. Following behind would come the Guards Armoured Division. Its task was to follow the leading armoured division and then swing to its left around Cagny and make for Vimont along the axis of the Caen–Vimont road and railway line. As the armoured brigades of these two divisions pushed southwards, their two infantry brigades would mop up the villages of the enemy behind them. 7th Armoured Division came next, heading for the ridge behind Bourguébus and Tilly la Campagne.

The charge of the armoured divisions led by 11th Armoured got under way at 07.45hrs as planned. The tanks of 29th Armoured Brigade headed through the gap to the left of Cuverville and Démouville and drove amongst enemy defenders demoralised by the bombing and shelling, making for the hamlet of Le Mesnil Frementel just beyond the first railway line. To their right, 159th Infantry Brigade dealt with the two villages that had been bypassed. The first railway was reached at 08.30hrs. Here there was a slight pause whilst the tanks regrouped and then, at around 08.50, a new rolling barrage began and the advance resumed. Ten minutes later the barrage ended. The tanks were moving beyond the range of the field artillery grouped on the other side of the Orne north-east of Caen. They were now on their own.

The tanks successfully reached and bypassed Le Mesnil Frementel. The brigade's accompanying motor battalion, 8th Rifle Brigade, dealt with the small village itself. They attacked Le Mesnil Frementel with the support of flail tanks and AVREs from 79th Armoured Division. The Shermans of 3rd Royal Tank Regiment and 2nd Fife and Forfar Yeomanry then pressed on over the second railway line, while 23rd Hussars watched the village of Cagny, waiting for the Guards Division to come up and assume responsibility for the left flank and attack the town.

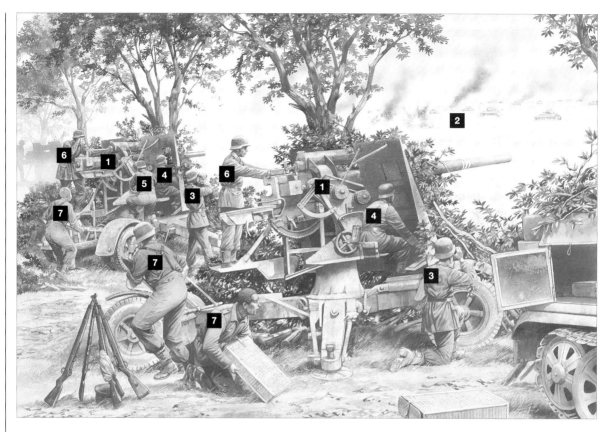

LUFTWAFFE 88MM GUNS ENGAGING BRITISH ARMOUR, CAGNY, 18 JULY 1944 (pages 78–79)

The large-scale bombing raids that preceded the armoured attacks of Operation Goodwood did great damage to German defences and troop concentrations. In the path of the armoured divisions the enemy defences were blasted apart and many of his guns and tanks completely destroyed. Some mobile units fared a little better and a few enemy gun batteries and tank companies were hidden in orchards and small woods away from towns and villages and so escaped the raids. Some of these were around Cagny and others were further to the south-west near the Bourguébus Ridge. One Luftwaffe anti-aircraft battery of four 88mm guns survived the bombing in Cagny and was intently waiting for the next raid. At around 10.00hrs on 18 July on the first day of Goodwood, the lead tanks of 11th Armoured Division had reached the ground to the west of Cagny and were advancing south-west over the Caen–Vimont railway line. At about this time the commander of 125th Panzergenadier Regiment, 21st Panzer Division, Oberst Hans von Luck, came up to Cagny to see the situation for himself. He was astonished to find that British armour had bypassed the town and was deploying in the open country to the south. Even worse, scores more tanks were swarming towards the town from the north. Nearby he found the Luftwaffe anti-aircraft battery and told the captain in command of the guns to move them to a nearby orchard and engage the British tanks. The young officer refused and said that his job was to watch for Allied planes and defend the industrial area

around Caen. 'Fighting tanks is your job', he told von Luck, 'I'm Luftwaffe.' Colonel von Luck drew his pistol, pointed it at the Luftwaffe captain and said, 'Either you are a dead man or you can earn yourself a medal.' The 88mm guns (1) were duly moved into the orchard and engaged the Shermans of 2nd Fife and Forfar Yeomanry (2) with devastating effect. The high muzzle-velocity and flat trajectory of the 88mm made it an excellent anti-tank weapon. Bearing in mind that the guns had a maximum range of 15,000 metres, they engaged the Shermans at what was virtually point-blank range. One after another the German shells struck home, knocking out the exposed tanks with horrifying regularity. The Sherman's notorious propensity to catch fire meant that most of them were left as burning wrecks. Each of the Flak 36 88mm Luftwaffe guns had an 11-man crew and although the entire crew is not visible, those shown here include the gun commander (3) the gun layer for traversing (4) seated on the right of the gun (the gunner's position was on a seat on the other side of the gun), the gun layer for elevation (5), the loader (6) and the ammunition handlers (7). This small detachment of Luftwaffe guns blunted the drive of 11th Armoured Division past Cagny and forced more and more of the tanks to veer to the north-west, slowing down their arrival over the railway line. The respite gained by the intervention of the battery of 88s allowed von Luck to move more troops into Cagny and organise a stubborn defence against the Guards Armoured Division when it arrived later in the day and attacked the town. (Peter Dennis)

German Panzergrenadiers from 21st Panzer Division moving towards the giant steelworks of Colombelles on the eastern outskirts of Caen. The maze of industrial buildings was the first main objective of Canadian 3rd Division on the opening day of Operation Goodwood. (Bundesarchiv 1011/721/0353/27A)

Several kilometres to the north, the bridges feeding the other two armoured divisions and the Canadians into the battle area were becoming congested. The traffic jams were causing the concentration of the follow-up armour and infantry to fall behind schedule. Further trouble was developing in the south for the survivors of the bombing were beginning to recover from their ordeal. Many tanks and guns had been shattered, and many hundreds of German troops had been killed, but officers and NCOs had now begun to galvanise their men into action and re-organise resistance to the British attack. Tanks and 88mm guns began to come into action.

Cagny had been totally destroyed by the heavy bombers, but the orchards and woods on the outskirts had escaped destruction, as had the gun areas to the south and east and the defences of Emiéville. These areas now overlooked the left flank of 11th Armoured Division's advance. A battery of Luftwaffe 88mm guns were brought into action in

Troops from 16th Luftwaffe Field Division and 21st Panzer Division seeking medical help at the aid station located beneath the industrial railway line that led into the steelworks at Colombelles. (Bundesarchiv 1011/721/0353/15A)

an orchard on the edge of Cagny and these guns began to wreak havoc on the tanks of 23rd Hussars exposed in the open fields.

The leading battalion of the Guards Division, 2nd Grenadier Guards, was at the same time trying to get forward to Cagny but was being engaged by enemy guns in Emiéville and progress was slow. Finally 1st Coldstream Guards moved to the right to get behind Cagny and attack towards Vimont along the line of the railway, but to do so had to go around Le Mesnil Frementel. This cut across the line of advance of 7th Armoured Division, which was now arriving in the area after being held up in the traffic jams in the rear. More congestion and more delay dogged the advance and it was midday before 23rd Hussars could leave Cagny to the Guards and rejoin the advance.

Earlier in the morning, the lead battalions of 11th Armoured Division had crossed the Caen–Vimont railway, making for the fortified villages of Soliers and Hubert Folie. This now put the tanks in open country in full view of the German guns on Bourguébus Ridge and in the fortified villages all around. All of these points had been outside the bombing areas and their defenders remained unaffected. British tank losses now soared as, devoid of cover and in perfect view of the enemy 88s on the ridge, the high-sided Shermans became easy targets. The medium guns on the other side of Caen did their best to provide supporting fire, but they were firing at their maximum range and their fall of shot had to be relayed back to the batteries by observers in slow flying aircraft. The Typhoons of 83 and 84 Groups flew a number of sorties throughout the day, but with so many targets it was difficult to give support to everyone. The 88mm guns continued blasting away throughout the day. Even more targets for them arrived in the area south of the railway when the tanks of the leading battalion of 7th Armoured Division began to close on their objectives, the villages beneath Bourguébus Ridge.

The flat, open ground over which 7th Armoured Division had to attack in the face of the German 88mm guns lining the Bourguébus Ridge. The picture is taken at La Hogue looking towards Cagny. (Ken Ford)

The Germans counterattacked at several points in the early afternoon. The tanks of 21st Panzer Division and the Tigers of schwere Panzer Abteilung 503 attacked towards Cagny and two groups from 1st SS-Panzer Division 'Leibstandarte' launched a counterstroke either side of the village of Bourguébus, the strongest of which was in the Tilly–La Hogue area. All three attacks were held by the British, but at great cost in armour. The whole battlefield was now littered with blazing and abandoned tanks. On every side, enemy anti-tank guns were picking off the British tanks, and the British infantry was meeting fierce resistance in each village and hamlet. The heavy bombing had shattered the enemy in the front line villages and even done great damage to his tanks and guns further back, but to the south, over the Caen–Vimont railway, and to the east of Cagny he remained as strong and determined as ever.

It took until early evening for 2nd Grenadier Guards and the infantry of 2nd Guards Brigade to finally take Cagny. The 2nd Irish Guards advanced a little further east near Frénouville against the tanks of 21st Panzer Division, but 1st Coldstream Guards could not make any progress along the embankment of the Caen–Vimont railway line. Further back along the railway towards Caen, 7th and 11th Armoured Divisions spent the remainder of the day trying to advance across the open fields towards their objectives. In this 7th Armoured was particularly unsuccessful. It had been held up for a long time crossing the bridges and its advance was delayed behind the tail of the Guards Armoured Division. By nightfall, it still only had the tanks of just one battalion, 5th Royal Tank Regiment, in action south of the railway.

On either flank of VIII Corps, the two infantry divisions made slow but steady progress southwards, protecting the armoured thrust and reducing enemy opposition. On the right of Canadian 3rd Division, Canadian 2nd Division began crossing the River Odon just to the south-west of Caen with its 4th Brigade, while 5th Brigade advanced across the River Orne in the city itself. By the morning of 19 July, Caen had almost been completely encircled by the Canadians, the only remaining gap included the industrial areas of Mondeville and Faubourg de Vaucelles.

German 503rd Heavy Tank Battalion with their new Tiger II tanks dispersed in a wood to the south of Caen. At the start of the Goodwood battle, the battalion just had its 1st Company equipped with these 70-ton monsters. They were amongst the first of their type to go into action against the Allies in the west. (Bundesarchiv 1011/721/0364/06)

At the end of the first day of Operation Goodwood, Second Army had clearly cracked the German line, its troops advancing five kilometres southwards. Casualties were acceptable at approximately 1,500 for the three corps. Tank losses were thought to be around 200. Enemy resistance was stiff, but a resumption of the armoured attack on the 19th would finally put the tanks onto their objectives and would open the way towards Falaise.

Von Kluge was aware of the great threat that the British attack posed and requested that OKW recall 12th SS-Panzer Division, which was en route to Lisieux for much-needed rest. He needed the 'Hitlerjugend' Division in the Vimont–Cagny area to support the depleted 21st Panzer Division who were trying to halt the British attack eastwards. During the attack, the Panzer division had been reduced to the equivalent of about one battalion. German 16th Luftwaffe Field Division had been virtually annihilated by the bombardment and its remnants had been placed under the control of 21st Panzer Division. The Germans had lost about 109 tanks that day.

On 19 July, Goodwood continued with the attacks down the flanks gaining more ground especially the Canadians around Caen. The armoured divisions spent some considerable time sorting themselves out and regrouping ready for a resumption of the advance. The traffic congestion in the rear was easing, although it had taken most of the night for 7th Armoured Division to get its infantry brigade over the river and forward. On the left the Guards Division edged its way past Cagny on either side and once again confronted 21st Panzer Division on the Vimont road and railway line, but could make little progress against the strong line of anti-tank guns ranged against it. Over on the right of VIII Corps advance, 11th Armoured Division once again braved the German 88s and spent the whole day trying to secure Bras and Hubert Folie. In the centre, the luckless 7th Armoured Division set out to take Four and Bourguébus. It succeeded in getting into the former village but was denied the latter.

At the end of 19 July a few more villages had been taken, but again the count in tanks destroyed was alarming. Almost 400 Allied tanks had now been knocked out. Every gain made had to endure the inevitable

Tiger IIs, known to the Allies as the 'King' or 'Royal' Tiger, going through their paces with 1st Company, 503rd Heavy Tank Battalion after they had been delivered to the battalion just before Operation Goodwood. The sleek Porsche turret and long 88mm gun gives the tank a most distinctive profile. (Bundesarchiv 1011/721/0397/34)

counterattack by the enemy to retrieve it. The Germans gave up nothing without a fight. Despite losing a series of villages below the Bourguébus ridge, Gen Eberbach of Panzer Group West was determined that his tanks should prevent the British from reaching the Caen–Falaise highway. He now ordered reinforcements across from II SS-Corps to help hold the line.

That afternoon, LtGen Dempsey realised that his armoured units would soon need to withdraw to rest and be re-equipped. The British left flank was where the German armour was most heavily concentrated, especially now that 12th SS-Panzer Division was coming back into the line, and it was here that the enemy was contesting any further advance most fiercely. Dempsey now ordered 49th Division and 33rd Armoured Brigade across from XXX Corps to take over this flank. He then ordered VIII Corps to take Bourguébus and hold its front until relieved by II Canadian Corps, making the Canadians responsible for the area from there westwards to the Orne.

On 20 July, the Guards consolidated their hold to the east of Cagny by taking Frénouville, but 12th SS-Panzer Division resisted all its attempts to push any further east towards Vimont. The 7th Armoured took Bourguébus, but could not advance beyond the village towards the Caen–Falaise road. Most of the fighting that day was done by Canadian II Corps as they tried to advance southwards to Verriers on the high ground to the west of the Caen–Falaise road. Barring the way were elements of 272nd Division and about 100 tanks from 1st SS-Panzer and 2nd Panzer divisions. It was very a difficult approach and after two days of fighting, the Canadians could progress no further than Ifs, three kilometres short of their objective.

Both sides now wanted to avoid launching a major attack to capture minor objectives and Goodwood was deemed to be over. The operation had failed in its main objective of securing the high ground that straddled the Caen–Falaise road, but it had improved Second Army's position on its eastern flank. Caen had been completely captured and finally removed from its dominating position in Montgomery's strategy. It had taken 36 days for his forces to capture the objective that he had planned to seize on D-Day.

AFTERMATH

General Montgomery has been the target of severe criticism for the way that the battle for Caen developed. The confident predictions that he had made before and after the invasion regularly failed to materialise. The ponderous slow battles and set-piece operations that gained just a few kilometres of new territory led to impatience in high places. The results of Epsom, Charnwood and Goodwood were disappointing when set against the cost in human life and the matériel expended in the attacks. Montgomery had his detractors, especially amongst the Americans and amongst senior RAF commanders who were anxious for space to build new airfields and were dismayed by the results on the ground after the colossal air raids they had laid on for the infantry. Criticism was levelled against him and questions were asked about his strategy. Some detractors wanted Montgomery sacked and Air Chief Marshal Sir Arthur Tedder urged Eisenhower to take over direct command of operations.

These limited results on the ground need to be seen in the context of Montgomery's strategy of drawing into Second Army's sector the bulk of the powerful German armoured units that might otherwise be redeployed to face the Americans further west. He insisted that as Commander 21st Army Group his policy had always been to make the break-out from Normandy with the Americans in the west, with mobile troops swinging east and west to take the Brittany peninsula and to get behind the forces

Canadian Sherman tank of the Sherbrooke Fusiliers from Canadian 2nd Armoured Brigade continues the advance through the dusty, broken villages of Normandy. (Harold Aitkin, NAC PA 162667)

that were stalling him in the east. That may be so, but the long slogging-matches along the Odon and Orne, and the high losses suffered by the British and Canadians, questioned whether or not his policy was the most effective use of Allied assets.

If one looks at the numbers of divisions involved in Normandy, his strategy did appear to be working. On 24 July, the Americans had 19 divisions in Normandy, of which four were armoured, facing German forces of around nine divisions, with two of these being Panzer divisions equipped with about 110 tanks. The British and Canadians had 14 divisions (three of them armoured) facing 14 German divisions of which seven were armoured and contained around 600 tanks, more than half of which were the more powerful Panthers and Tigers.

The slow nature of British Second Army's progress in Normandy has attracted a lot of criticism, but what should not be overlooked is the equally slow progress achieved by US First Army. After the capture of the Cotentin peninsula on 29 June, Bradley was ordered to prepare for his big break-out battle, Operation Cobra. Just as Montgomery could not capture Caen to gain room to manoeuvre, Bradley proved equally unable to seize St Lô. His forces were attacking through particularly thick areas of the Normandy bocage and enemy resistance there was fierce. Montgomery set the ambitious date of 3 July for Bradley to launch Cobra, but this soon proved to be out of the question. On 10 July, Bradley told Montgomery that he

could not start until 20 July. Montgomery responded to the delay by launching the attacks along the Odon made by XII and XXX Corps on 15 July and Operation Goodwood on 18 July, in order to keep enemy armour away from the Americans.

In the event, it was not until 25 July that Bradley finally made his attack. Operation Cobra was then launched in the same manner that Montgomery had launched Goodwood: a massive aerial bombardment and an attack by armoured forces on a relatively narrow front. After two days of heavy fighting the enemy started to withdraw and a gap began to open in the line. To keep the pressure on, Montgomery attacked again in the east, this time with Canadian II Corps. The objective once more was the Caen–Falaise road. Enemy reaction was predictable and savage. The Canadians were stopped by determined resistance put up by elements of 1st SS, 9th SS, 10th SS and 21st Panzer Divisions.

With the German armour still tied to Montgomery's sector of the line, the Americans began to pour southwards and the whole Allied front began to pivot around Caumont. By 31 July, Avranches had been reached and the way into Brittany was open. On 1 August, General George Patton's Third Army became operational. At the same time General Courtney Hodges took over US First Army and Bradley became Commander 12th Army Group, finally freeing himself from Montgomery's control. Montgomery had, however, already taken responsibility for a new army, as on 23 July General Henry Crerar's First Canadian Army had become operational. Crerar took British I Corps under command and was given responsibility for the eastern sector of the British line.

Patton now unleashed his mobile forces to operate freely in the enemy's rear. On 5 August, Nantes near the mouth of the River Loire was reached, isolating Brittany from the rest of France. Von Kluge was alarmed by these moves and released troops from the eastern sector. He sent five divisions westwards in an effort to stem the tide, but it was too late. Patton and his men were now rampant, motoring tens of kilometres each day against negligible opposition.

A 25-pdr field gun of the Royal Canadian Artillery firing in support of an attack by Canadian 3rd Division. The gun has been dug into a pit to give it and its crew some protection from enemy counter-battery fire. (Ken Bell, NAC 115569)

In the north-east, Montgomery was still confronted by the bulk of the German armour and difficult terrain. On 30 July, after shifting the main weight of his forces to the centre of his sector, Montgomery began his break-out battle from around Caumont, heading for Vire. Leading the attack was VIII Corps, which had been switched from one side of the battlefield to the other. The countryside that its troops had to contend with was the *bocage* at its worst and progress once again was slow. The same was true for XII and XXX Corps. The dense countryside of tree-covered hills and steep valleys, small fields and narrow lanes was perfect defensive terrain and the enemy used it superbly, resisting each Allied advance until the British were almost upon them before melting away in the undergrowth. Whilst the Americans were grabbing the headlines, the British were still slogging away at the enemy at close quarters as they had done since arriving in Normandy.

Two more armoured divisions now arrived in Normandy to bring Montgomery's forces to a position of strength that he was never again to achieve. Canadian 4th Armoured Division and 1st Polish Armoured Division were dispatched to the east of the Orne ready for the next attempt to break through to Falaise. All along the front the enemy was giving way in the face of overwhelming odds. Hitler was furious and in a fit of extreme optimism or madness ordered 1st SS-Panzer, 10th SS-Panzer, 2nd Panzer and 116th Panzer divisions, together with 84th and 363rd Infantry divisions, to counterattack the Americans at Mortain on 7 August. Not surprisingly, given the strength of the Americans and the dominance of Allied air power, the attack failed with heavy German losses.

The results of the disastrous Mortain counterattack were felt all along the German line. Everywhere it started to recoil and fall back. The Americans were sweeping south-east to get behind German Seventh Army at the same time that British Second and Canadian First Armies were attacking from the north. There was still much fighting to be done, but the trap was closing inexorably around all the German forces in Normandy, gradually forcing them into a pocket between Falaise and Argentan. On 19 August, this pocket was finally closed and those disorganised Germans that escaped death or capture were fleeing pell-mell towards the River Seine in the east.

THE BATTLEFIELD TODAY

The Calvados area of Normandy has long since returned to the prime agricultural area that it was before war descended on it with a vengeance in June 1944. The countryside around Caen is once more a patchwork of small fields, high hedges and sunken lanes, intermeshed with gentle rolling hills covered with summer corn. All the small villages with names that once resonated with death to the men who fought for their possession have been rebuilt. In 1944 their destruction was complete, with barely a house or wall standing.

The countryside has few prominent landmarks of any note and it may come as something of a surprise to a visitor to the battlefield that so many men should die for possession of this insignificant village or that diminutive river. Little now remains to remind anyone of the struggle that took place here. The armchair historian may, in his mind's eye, see Hill 112 as a towering vantage point that stamped its significance on the battlefield. It comes as something of a disappointment to find that its rounded bare slopes merge with other rounded bare slopes to a point that it could easily be passed by, were it not for the granite monument to 43rd Wessex Division near its summit. The memorial commemorates the 2,000 casualties suffered in the failed attempt to capture the hill. Nearby stands a Churchill tank with its gun pointing towards the small wood on the summit that 5th Cornwalls took and lost. It is not a veteran of the battle, but a rusty relic from an English firing range, repainted and tidied up as a further memorial to the tanks and men who were lost on the hillside. Between the two is the battered Croix de Filandrières, a wayside Calvary that witnessed the carnage that took place around it in July 1944. Three kilometres or so to the north is the River Odon. The tiny bridge over the river at Tourmauville, which was seized by 2nd Argyll and Sutherland Highlanders during Epsom, is still there carrying present-day traffic where once tanks poured across into the Scottish bridgehead. If the road is followed northwards a short distance towards Tourville, you will find the impressive monument to 15th Scottish Division standing tall over the battlefield.

Few of the more tangible remains of the battle for Caen are to be seen. There are one or two German bunkers still existing around Carpiquet airfield, the most accessible of which is the prominent concrete command post situated right outside the passenger terminal. Virtually all the other fortifications used in the battle were trench systems and earthworks that were long ago filled in by landowners so that the ground could be returned to agricultural use.

The city of Caen has been rebuilt and is now once again the prosperous regional capital of Calvados. With almost 75 per cent of the buildings destroyed in the Allied blitz of June and July 1944, it seems almost miraculous that some of Caen's most magnificent heritage sites still exist today. Dominating the city centre is its massive chateau, with strong walls

A restored Churchill tank acts as a memorial to the men from all the units who died in the battles to take possession of Hill 112. The tank stands beside the road from Caen to Evrecy looking towards 'Cornwall Wood' on the summit of the notorious hill. (Ken Ford)

made of the creamy local stone quarried from sites all over the battlefield. The chateau became the headquarters of GenLt Richter when he was forced out of his bunker at La Folie. Other German occupation forces also took shelter here. William the Conqueror's medieval fortress still stands proud over the bustling city life that goes on around it. The great Norman king now lies nearby in the ancient Abbaye aux Hommes, with his queen buried in the Abbaye aux Dames, both buildings having survived the bombing.

On western the outskirts of Caen, near the Péripherique ring road that circles the city, is the Mémorial Musée Pour la Paix, the Memorial Museum for Peace. The museum occupies the site of a former stone quarry at La Folie where GenLt Richter, Commander 716th Infantry Division, had his headquarters on D-Day. His underground bunker has been incorporated into the museum's Nobel Gallery. The museum welcomes visitors from all over the world and has excellent facilities, including a large reference library and an impressive bookshop.

On the eastern side of the city, a drive through the ground covered by the Goodwood battle is a sobering experience. The villages that were torn apart by bombers and shellfire have been rebuilt and the fields returned to agriculture, but the layout of the battlefield remains the same. The wide flat areas between the villages marked it out as good tank country with room to manoeuvre armoured formations. It was also excellent countryside for well-sited anti-tank guns. Look to the south-west and the long, low silhouette of the Bourguébus Ridge can be seen running across the near horizon. Drive up through Bourguébus and Tilly la Campagne and then look back across the ground over which the armoured battalions advanced in their tanks and you can easily see why so many of them were picked off by the 88mm guns that were sited along the ridge.

Cemeteries are scattered throughout the area, testament to the severity of the fighting. Most of the German dead who were killed in the Caen battles are buried in the cemeteries at Cambes, near Isigny or at Marigny-la-Chapelle, near St Lô. Canadian dead are buried in the Canadian War Cemetery at Bény sur Mer just inland from Courseulles. British dead lie in various Commonwealth War Cemeteries dotted throughout the Normandy countryside at Sannerville, St Manvieu, Tilly, Juvigny, Rauray and Bayeux, but perhaps the most poignant of them all is at Secqueville en Bessin, situated about 14km due south of Courseulles sur Mer and the coast. This must be the most exposed and desolate of all the Normandy cemeteries, stuck way out from any village surrounded by open wind-swept fields. Inside the graveyard all is neat, tidy and peaceful as ever, but its isolated location means that it sadly gets very few visitors. The 99 British burials here, of which one is unknown, are of men from the West Country county regiments who made up 43rd Wessex Division killed during Operation Jupiter, the battle to take Hill 112. Why these men should have been brought here to this isolated spot 16km from Hill 112 for burial is a mystery. Alongside the Wessexmen are the graves of 18 German soldiers. Once enemies, 117 young men now lie in their graves alongside each other in a corner of a foreign land.

ORDER OF BATTLE

British & Commonwealth forces

21st Army Group – General Sir Bernard Law Montgomery
British Second Army – Lieutenant-General Sir Miles Dempsey

D-DAY, 6 JUNE 1944

British I Corps – Lieutenant-General John Crocker

3rd Division – Major-General Tom Rennie
   8th Brigade – Brigadier E. Cass
   9th Brigade – Brigadier J.C. Cunningham
   185th Brigade – Brigadier K.P. Smith

6th Airborne Division – Major-General Richard N. Gale
   3rd Parachute Brigade – Brigadier James Hill
   5th Parachute Brigade – Brigadier Nigel Poett
   6th Airlanding Brigade – Brigadier Hugh Kindersley

Canadian 3rd Division – Major-General R.F.L. Keller
   7th Brigade – Brigadier H.W. Foster
   8th Brigade – Brigadier K.G. Blackader
   9th Brigade – Brigadier D.G. Cunningham

British 27th Armoured Brigade – Brigadier G.E. Prior Palmer
Canadian 2nd Armoured Brigade – Brigadier Wyman
British 1st Special Service Brigade – Brigadier Lord Lovat
British 4th Special Service Brigade – Brigadier B.W. Leicester

British XXX Corps – Lieutenant-General Gerard Bucknall

British 50th (Northumbrian) Division – Major-General D.A.H. Graham
   56th Brigade – Brigadier E.C. Pepper
   69th Brigade – Brigadier F.Y.C. Knox
   151st Brigade – Brigadier R.H. Senior
   231st Brigade – Brigadier Sir A.B.G. Stanier

8th Armoured Brigade – Brigadier H.J.B. Cracroft

OPERATION EPSOM

British VIII Corps – Lieutenant-General Sir Richard O'Connor

15th Scottish Division – Major-General G.H.A. MacMillan
   44th Lowland Brigade – Brigadier Douglas Money
   46th Highland Brigade – Brigadier C.M. Darber
   227th Highland Brigade – Brigadier E.C. Colville

43rd Wessex Division – Major-General G.I. Thomas
   129th Brigade – Brigadier G.H.L. Mole
   130th Brigade – Brigadier N.D. Leslie
   214th Brigade – Brigadier H. Essame

53rd Welsh Division – Major-General R.K. Ross
   71st Brigade – Brigadier V. Blomfield
   158th Brigade – Brigadier S.O. Jones
   160th Brigade – Brigadier C.F.C. Coleman

11th Armoured Division – Major-General G.P.B. 'Pip' Roberts
   29th Armoured Brigade – Brigadier C.B.C. Harvey
   159th Infantry Brigade – Brigadier J.G. Sandie[2]

4th Armoured Brigade – Brigadier J. Currie
31st Tank Brigade – Brigadier G.S. Knight

British XXX Corps – Lieutenant-General Gerard Bucknall

49th West Riding Division – Major-General E.H. Barker
   70th Brigade – Brigadier E.C. Cooke-Collis
   146th Brigade – Brigadier J.F. Walker
   147th Brigade – Brigadier E.R. Mahony[3]

50th Northumbrian Division – Major-General D.A.H. Graham
   (see above for constituent units)

7th Armoured Division – Major-General George Erskine
   22nd Armoured Brigade – Brigadier R.N. Hinde
   131st Infantry Brigade – Brigadier M.S. Ekins[4]

OPERATION CHARNWOOD

British I Corps – Lieutenant-General John Crocker

3rd Division – Major-General L.G. Whistler
   (see above for constituent units)

59th Staffordshire Division – Major-General L.O. Lyne
   176th Brigade – Brigadier R.W.H. Fryer
   177th Brigade – Brigadier M. Elrington
   197th Brigade – Brigadier J. Lingham

Canadian 3rd Division – Major-General R.F.L. Keller
   (see above for constituent units)

OPERATION GOODWOOD

British I Corps

3rd Division [rank and initials] Whistler
   (see above for constituent units)

6th Airborne Division – Major-General Richard N. Gale
   (see above for constituent units)

51st Highland Division – Major-General C. Bullen-Smith
   152nd Brigade – Brigadier A.J.H. Cassels
   153rd Brigade – Brigadier H. Murray
   154th Brigade – Brigadier J. Oliver

British VIII Corps

7th Armoured Division – Major-General George Erskine
   (see above for constituent units)

11th Armoured Division – Major-General 'Pip' Roberts
   (see above for constituent units)

Guards Armoured Division – Major-General A.H.S. Adair
   5th Guards Armoured Brigade – Brigadier N.W. Gwatkin
   32nd Guards Brigade – Brigadier G.F. Johnson

Canadian II Corps – Lieutenant-General Guy Simmonds

Canadian 2nd Division – Major-General C. Foulkes
   4th Brigade – Brigadier Sherwood Lett
   5th Brigade
   6th Brigade

Canadian 3rd Division – Major-General R.F.L. Keller
   (see above for constituent units)

Canadian 2nd Armoured Brigade – Brigadier Wyman

NOTES
2 Replaced by Brigadier J.B. Churcher on 27 June 1944.
3 Until 4 July 1944, then Brigadier H. Wood..
4 Until 2 July 1944, then Brigadier E.C. Pepper.

German forces – Caen sector

In the Caen sector German forces remained largely on the defensive throughout June and July 1944. With units moving rapidly from sector to sector, responding to particular Allied attacks or short-term crises in certain sectors of the line, the command and organisational structure was fluid. The order of battle shown below is thus representational. All those divisions shown were engaged against the British or Canadian forces around Caen, but did not necessarily serve with the particular corps shown at the same time.

C-in-C (West) – Generalfeldmarschall Gerd von Rundstedt[5]

Army Group B – Generalfeldmarschall Erwin Rommel[6]
German Seventh Army – Generaloberst Friedrich Dollmann[7]

Panzer Group West – General der Panzertruppen Geyr von Schweppenburg[8]

LXXXIV Corps – General der Artillerie Erich Marcks[9] (killed 12 June 1944?? Who then?)
716th Infantry Division – Generalleutnant Wilhelm Richter
   726th Grenadier Regiment – Oberst Korfes
   736th Grenadier Regiment – Oberst Krug

352nd Infantry Division – Generalleutnant Dietrich Kraiss
   914th Grenadier Regiment – Oberst Heyna
   915th Grenadier Regiment – Oberst Meyer
   916th Grenadier Regiment – Oberst Goth

I SS-Panzer Corps – SS-Obergruppenführer Josef 'Sepp' Dietrich
1st SS-Panzer Division 'Leibstandarte SS Adolf Hitler' – SS-Brigadeführer Theodor Wisch
   1st SS-Panzer Regiment
   1st SS-Panzergrenadier Regiment
   2nd SS-Panzergrenadier Regiment

12th SS-Panzer Division 'Hitlerjugend' – SS-Brigadeführer Fritz Witt[10]
   12th SS-Panzer Regiment – SS-Standartenführer Max Wünsche
   25th SS-Panzergrenadier Regiment – SS-Standartenführer Kurt Meyer
   26th SS-Panzergrenadier Regiment – SS-Standartenführer Wilhelm Möhnke

21st Panzer Division – Generalmajor Edgar Feuchtinger
   100th (later 22nd) Panzer Regiment – Oberst Oppeln-Bronikowski
   125th Panzergrenadier Regiment – Oberst Hans von Luck
   192nd Panzergrenadier Regiment – Oberst Rauch

Panzer Lehr Division – Generalleutnant Fritz Bayerlein/Generalmajor Hyazinth Strachwitz
   130th Panzer Regiment
   901st Panzergrenadier Regiment
   902nd Panzergrenadier Regiment

272nd Infantry Division – Generalleutnant Friedrich Schack
   980th Grenadier Regiment
   981st Grenadier Regiment
   982nd Grenadier Regiment

II SS-Panzer Corps – SS-Obergruppenführer Paul Hausser/ SS-Obergruppenführer Wilhelm Bittrich
2nd SS-Panzer Division 'Das Reich' – SS-Oberführer Heinz Lammerding
   2nd SS-Panzer Regiment
   3rd SS-Panzergrenadier Regiment 'Deutschland'
   4th SS-Panzergrenadier Regiment 'Der Führer'

9th SS-Panzer Division 'Hohenstaufen' – SS-Oberführer Thomas Müller/SS-Oberführer Sylvester Stadler
   9th SS-Panzer Regiment
   19th Panzergrenadier Regiment
   20th SS-Panzergrenadier Regiment

10th SS-Panzer Division 'Frundsberg' – SS-Brigadeführer Heinz Harmel
   10th SS-Panzer Regiment
   21st SS-Panzergrenadier Regiment
   22nd SS-Panzergrenadier Regiment

277th Infantry Divison – Generalleutnant Albert Praum
   989th Grenadier Regiment
   990th Grenadier Regiment
   991st Grenadier Regiment

8th Werfer Brigade

XLVII Panzer Corps – General von Funck
2nd Panzer Division – Generalleutnant Baron Heinrich von Lüttwitz
   3rd Panzer Regiment
   2nd Panzergrenadier Regiment
   304th Panzergrenadier Regiment

276th Infantry Division – Generalleutnant Curt Badinski
   986th Grenadier Regiment
   987th Grenadier Regiment
   988th Grenadier Regiment

326th Infantry Division — Generalleutnant Viktor von Drabich-Wächter
   751st Grenadier Regiment
   752nd Grenadier Regiment
   753rd Grenadier Regiment

LXXXI Corps – General der Panzertruppen Adolf Kuntzen
711th Infantry Division – Generalleutnant Josef Reichert
   731st Grenadier Regiment
   744th Grenadier Regiment

346th Infantry Division – Generalleutnant Erich Diester
   857th Grenadier Regiment
   858th Grenadier Regiment

7th Werfer Brigade

LXXXVI Corps – General der Infanterie Hans von Obstfelder
16th Luftwaffe Field Division – Generalleutnant Karl Sievers
   31st Field Infantry Regiment
   32nd Field Infantry Regiment
   45th Field Infantry Regiment

346th Infantry Division
(see above for details)

711th Infantry Division
(see above for details)

9th Werfer Brigade

NOTES
5 Replaced by Generalfeldmarschall Günther von Kluge on 2 July 1944
6 Generalfeldmarschall Günther von Kluge took command of Army Group B after Rommel was wounded on 17 July 1944.
7 Following Dollmann's suicide on 29 June 1944, SS-Obergruppenführer Paul Hausser.
8 General der Panzertruppen Heinrich Eberbach from 4 July 1944.
9 Killed 12 June 1944, then General der Artillerie Wilhelm Fahrbacher.
10 Killed by Allied shellfire 14 June 1944.

The tiny harbour at Port en Bessin was rendered unusable to the Allies for some weeks as a result of demolitions carried out by the Germans as they left. Here a small freighter blocks one of the berths. (IWM B5395)

BIBLIOGRAPHY

Anon, *Operation 'Neptune' Landings in Normandy, June 1944*, HMSO (London, 1994)

Anon *The Story of the 79th Armoured Division*, Privately printed, (1946)

Carell, Paul, *Invasion – They're Coming!*, George Harrap (London, 1962)

D'Este, Carlo, *Decision in Normandy*, Collins (London, 1983)

Ellis, Maj L.F., *Victory In The West Vol. 1*, HMSO (London, 1962)

Ford, Ken, *D-Day 1944 (3): Sword Beach & the British Airborne Landings*, Osprey (Oxford, 2002)

Ford, Ken, *D-Day 1944 (4): Gold and Juno Beaches*, Osprey (Oxford, 2002)

Ford, Ken, *Battlezone Normandy: Juno Beach*, Sutton Publishing (Stroud, 2004)

Hastings, Max, *Overlord*, Michael Joseph (London, 1984)

Keegan, John, *Six Armies in Normandy*, Jonathan Cape (London, 1982)

McKee, Alexander, *Caen: Anvil of Victory*, Souvenir Press (1964)

Meyer, Hubert, *The History of the 12th SS Panzer Division 'Hitlerjugend'*, J.J. Fedorowicz (Winnipeg, Canada, 1994)

Montgomery, Field Marshal Sir Bernard, *Normandy to the Baltic*, Hutchinson (1947)

Perrigault, Jean-Claude, *21. Panzer-Division*, Heimdal (Bayeux, France 2002)

Scarfe, Norman, *Assault Division*, Collins (London, 1947)

Stacey, Col C.P, *The Canadian Army 1939–45*, Ministry of National Defence

Commonwealth War Graves Commission's cemetery at Bayeux where many of those British soldiers who died in the battles for Caen are buried. (Ken Ford)

INDEX